Reframing Education as a Public and Common Good

"Rita Locatelli has a brilliant understanding of education as a global common good. After the wreckage of society by market automata and the nativist assault on solidarity, our crucial task is to rebuild institutions based on community and recognition of our shared human and ecological destiny. The author brings education to the front of our thinking about civic democracy. Her book is also immensely readable. Strongly recommended!"
—Professor Simon Marginson, *University of Oxford, UK*, and Director of the *ESRC/OFSRE Centre for Global Higher Education*

"This book will become an essential resource for anyone interested in education governance. By drawing on a wide range of global examples, the author provides an in-depth and timely discussion around the idea of education as a public good."
—Rille Raaper, *Durham University, UK*

"While much has been written on the growing global trend towards privatization, this book rightly situates a critique of that trend within a broader examination of the public and the common good. As is appropriate, confronting efforts to privatize education should be met with a consideration of the implications for the common good and, thankfully, Locatelli provides us with the necessary language, understanding, and global contextualization that is much needed towards those efforts."
—T. Jameson Brewer, *University of North Georgia, USA*

Rita Locatelli

Reframing Education as a Public and Common Good

Enhancing Democratic Governance

palgrave
macmillan

Rita Locatelli
International Research Centre on Global Citizenship Education
University of Bologna
Bologna, Italy

ISBN 978-3-030-24800-0   ISBN 978-3-030-24801-7   (eBook)
https://doi.org/10.1007/978-3-030-24801-7

© The Editor(s) (if applicable) and The Author(s) 2019
This work is subject to copyright. All rights are solely and exclusively licensed by the Publisher, whether the whole or part of the material is concerned, specifically the rights of translation, reprinting, reuse of illustrations, recitation, broadcasting, reproduction on microfilms or in any other physical way, and transmission or information storage and retrieval, electronic adaptation, computer software, or by similar or dissimilar methodology now known or hereafter developed.
The use of general descriptive names, registered names, trademarks, service marks, etc. in this publication does not imply, even in the absence of a specific statement, that such names are exempt from the relevant protective laws and regulations and therefore free for general use.
The publisher, the authors and the editors are safe to assume that the advice and information in this book are believed to be true and accurate at the date of publication. Neither the publisher nor the authors or the editors give a warranty, express or implied, with respect to the material contained herein or for any errors or omissions that may have been made. The publisher remains neutral with regard to jurisdictional claims in published maps and institutional affiliations.

This Palgrave Macmillan imprint is published by the registered company Springer Nature Switzerland AG.
The registered company address is: Gewerbestrasse 11, 6330 Cham, Switzerland

Acknowledgements

The drafting of this book has been a challenging yet extraordinary experience, and I owe much gratitude and appreciation to the many persons with whom I had the fortune to share this journey.

My first thanks go to Palgrave Macmillan, especially to Rebecca Wyde and Eleanor Christie for having entrusted me with this important project.

I really wish to thank Simon Marginson, who ensured that this book became a reality, for his continued encouragement and appreciation.

My sincere thanks go to Sobhi Tawil who, since my first experience at UNESCO Education Research and Foresight, has inspired me to think in new ways.

I owe special thanks to Pamela Wigley for her meticulous, patient, and professional assistance in the proof-reading of this book.

I am particularly indebted to my dearest friends and to my family for their unconditional support.

Contents

1 Introduction   1

2 Different Interpretations of the Concept of Education As a Public Good in International Discourse   15

3 Education: A Private or Public Good?   33

4 A Changing Global Education Landscape: Growing Involvement of Non-State Actors   51

5 Reframing the Concept of Education As a Public Good   91

6 Education As a Common Good   117

7 Going Global: Education As a Global Common Good   149

8 Conclusion   171

Index   185

List of Figures

Fig. 3.1	The expanding public domain. (Source: Drache 2001)	47
Fig. 4.1	Classification of public and private welfare activity. (Source: Burchardt et al. 1999)	57
Fig. 4.2	Percentage of enrolment in primary education in private institutions (UIS database)	63
Fig. 4.3	Percentage of enrolment in secondary education in private institutions (UIS database)	64
Fig. 4.4	Total funding for education by source. (Source: UIS and IIEP 2016)	66
Fig. 5.1	Role of the State according to combinations of lower and higher levels of democracy and of private actors' involvement	97
Fig. 6.1	Education as a common good implies an integrated approach	141

List of Tables

Table 2.1	Levels of interpretation of the concept of education as a public good in education development discourse	28
Table 3.1	Private and public goods	36
Table 4.1	Provision versus funding in educational services	55
Table 4.2	The multifaceted phenomenon of privatization	58
Table 5.1	Public-good versus market-based approach	95
Table 5.2	Roles and levels of responsibility of the State in education	102
Table 6.1	Public goods versus common goods	126

1

Introduction

Over the course of the last few decades, education has increasingly been referred to as a public good in education development and human rights discourse. The education-related Goal 4 of the 2030 Agenda for Sustainable Development[1]—*Ensure inclusive and equitable quality education and promote lifelong learning opportunities for all*—outlined in the Incheon Declaration,[2] is grounded on long-established foundational principles that refer to the recognition of education as a human right and as a public good (UNESCO 2015a: 5). This vision is also recalled and further detailed in the Framework for Action[3] which outlines how to translate into practice the commitments envisaged in the Education 2030 agenda. It is stated that "Education is a public good, of which the state is the duty bearer" (UNESCO 2015a: 10).

---

[1] United Nations. 2015. *Transforming our world: the 2030 Agenda for Sustainable Development.* New York, United Nations (UN General Assembly Resolution 70/1).

[2] The Incheon Declaration *Education 2030: Towards inclusive and equitable quality education and lifelong learning for all* was adopted at the World Education Forum held in Incheon (Republic of Korea), 19–22 May 2015.

[3] UNESCO. 2015. *Education 2030 Incheon Declaration and Framework for Action: Towards Inclusive and Equitable Quality Education and Lifelong Learning for All.* Paris, UNESCO.

© The Author(s) 2019
R. Locatelli, *Reframing Education as a Public and Common Good,*
https://doi.org/10.1007/978-3-030-24801-7_1

On the basis of a general interpretation of the theory of public goods, as developed by the economists Samuelson and Musgrave,[4] the notion of education as a public good aims to reaffirm the primary responsibility of the State in ensuring that *all* children have access to education by directly providing or financing educational opportunities, particularly for the duration of compulsory education. Indeed, the first target of Sustainable Development Goal 4 (SDG4) further stipulates the provision of 12 years of free public primary and secondary education of which at least 9 years should be compulsory. The role of the State is considered fundamental since, as also envisaged in legal frameworks underpinning the right to education, it is the main actor that has to safeguard the respect of principles of equality of opportunity, equity and inclusion. This is all the more important given the need to ensure that discrimination is avoided, and marginalized or underprivileged groups also have access to quality education opportunities. In this perspective, States have a key role in safeguarding the public interest in education and are expected to directly provide or finance educational opportunities, especially at the basic and compulsory level.

The leading role of the State in educational policies and practices is however increasingly being questioned, largely as a result of the changing dynamics in the global educational landscape. This is characterized by the greater involvement of non-state actors[5] in educational policy and provision, as well as by the growing scale of for-profit education at all levels. These changes are undoubtedly the result of several interconnected trends that have seen the increasing involvement of private actors in the funding and delivery of education opportunities. One of the main trends can be attributed to the "remarkable and unprecedented expansion in access to education at all levels" that has occurred worldwide over the last two decades and which has resulted in greater pressures on public financing (UNESCO 2015b: 13). The resulting public sector capacity constraints have created numerous opportunities for non-state actors to get involved in the sector. Under the trends of education privatization lies the assumption

---

[4] See the works by Samuelson (1954) and Musgrave (1959).

[5] Throughout this book, the term "non-state actors" refers to all individuals or organizations that are wholly or partly independent from state governments. These include households, the private sector, civil society organizations, non-governmental organizations, teachers unions and regional, multilateral and international organizations.

that the private sector can provide better quality education and, when functioning as corporate or business organizations, can be more efficient also in the management of the education system. The growing collaboration with the private sector, and the consequently increasing diversification of actors involved at different levels of the education endeavour, has contributed to the blurring of boundaries between the public and the private. Within this context, it has been argued that the multifaceted process of privatization may undermine the relevance of the concept of the public good as a guiding principle for educational governance (UNESCO 2015c).

Moreover, the principle of education as a public good, traditionally defined within the contours of the nation-state, is further challenged by the progressive shift in the locus of decision-making, from a national to a global level. Indeed, regional and global initiatives in education are increasingly influencing national education policies and practices, sometimes encouraging the development of for-profit private education. At the same time, the trends of globalization and liberalization of markets have encouraged a more utilitarian and individualistic approach to education, based on the human capital theory and on rates of return on investment in education, also promoting private engagement in the sector. Rooted in neo-liberal ideologies, these dynamics enhance the adoption of free-market logics, notably those of choice, economic competition and performance. In this perspective, education is conceived merely as an individual socio-economic investment and, therefore, as a marketable, consumable good (Macpherson et al. 2014). Indeed, it has been argued that the introduction of market mechanisms in the education sector may call into question specific aspects of the properties of public goods, since market involvement can lead to some forms of exclusion, thus making education more similar to a private good (Kohlrausch and Leuze 2007).

1.1 Rationale

The issue of determining the extent to which the private sector should be engaged in education has been at the centre of an intense debate in the education development field. The growing trend of the involvement of for-profit actors in the sector has raised important issues with regard to the nature and purposes of education itself, and with regard to the consequences for societal development in general. Whether education is considered to be a public or private marketable good is related to two competing visions of the purposes of education (Labaree 2011). It raises important questions about both the organization of education and the governance of education systems. This is related to the respective roles of the State, the market and other stakeholders involved in education and the distribution of power that exists among them.

Questions have been raised regarding the viability of the traditional role of the State in education—one that commits States to the primary responsibility to directly fund, provide, monitor, and regulate education opportunities. Indeed, the increasing demand for education at all levels has contributed, along with the Education for All and the Millennium Development Goals global agendas, to an expansion of access to education and to the lengthening of the average duration of schooling across the world. The growth in enrolment, also resulting from the significant global demographic changes, has generated greater pressures on public schooling systems in terms of both funding and delivery of education opportunities, contributing to the "failure" of governments to provide quality, basic education to all their citizens.

It has been argued that the notion of public good—and the role of the public and private sector in achieving this—"will probably always be, and should be, a contested subject" (Mansbridge 1998: 4). In a context characterized by increased complexity and by the blurring of boundaries between the public and the private, it is necessary to revisit the concept of education as a public good in order to determine the policy implications with regard to the role of the State in the governance of education systems.

Moreover, given "the peculiar nature of education", which involves both public and private interests (Levin 2000), and the difficulty in making a clear-cut distinction between the public and private sphere in this field (Robertson et al. 2012), it seems more and more difficult to reconcile the economic private purposes with the public-good aspects of education. Since private providers—also for-profit ones—may be expected to provide public goods (Olson 1965), and that forms of privatization and of marketization are possible also thanks to the direct intervention of

1 Introduction 5

the State, it is becoming increasingly challenging to ensure that economic investments of for-profit actors in the field of education are not guided by mere opportunity for business expansion but are principally aimed at contributing to the public interest.

Since systems of governance for the delivery of education are becoming more complex, it is necessary to rethink the principles that should guide such governance. In this respect, it is more and more evident that a "blanket defence of the public sector, as it is or was, over and against the inroads of privatisation, is untenable. [...] There is no going back to a past in which the public sector as a whole worked well and worked fairly in the interests of all learners. There was no such past" (Ball 2007: i). As acknowledged by many scholars, in order to address the long-standing crisis in education systems, there is need for a shift in culture—a transformative change in order to significantly revisit and reshape the way of functioning of public institutions themselves (UNESCO 2016; Apple and Beane 1995, 2007; Hursh 2016; Tedesco 1995).

Since such a challenge is not merely a question of economics but of democracy (Reich 2015), reframing the concept of education as a public good should take into consideration both economic and political perspectives which focus on the institutional regulation of goods (Kohlrausch and Leuze 2007). As argued by the historian and social critic Tony Judt (2010), "the choice will no longer be between the state and the market, but between two sorts of states. It is thus incumbent upon us to reconceive the role of government. If we do not, others will" (p. 9).

1.2 The Object and Purpose of the Book

The new global educational landscape requires a clearer understanding of why the principle of education as a public good has constantly appeared in education development discourse over the last few decades and what it possibly means today in light of the changing dynamics in the governance of education both at the national and at the global level. This is all the more important given the renewed commitment and the ambitious goal of the international community to ensure that "all girls and boys complete free, equitable and quality primary and secondary education leading to relevant and effective learning outcomes"[6].

This book maps out trends in, and the rationales for, private engagement in schooling, including the development of public–private partnerships in education, the controversial growth of low-fee private schools in the global South, and the emergence of what some have termed the "Global Education Industry"[7]. It examines how market approaches have been reshaping state institutions and state–education relations (Robertson and Verger 2012). This is necessary in order to understand what the implications of the growing trends of privatization and marketization with regard to the role of the State in education are. It also aims at identifying potential challenges that for-profit business engagement in education poses to the role of the State and to democratic policy-making, democratic governance and the societal collective purposes of education.

It takes into consideration how the principle of education as a public good may be reframed in order to address the challenges that arise from the governance of education systems in a context characterized by greater complexity and uncertainty, especially in light of the increasing variety of stakeholders involved in education. This may be useful in order to understand the conditions under which for-profit participation undermines or contributes to the aim of a public-good approach, that of ensuring free and quality education for all. Defining the role of the State will be necessary to avoid the risk that "business interests creep into the formulation of aims and strategy" (Draxler 2014: 24), thus leading to the privatization of the educational governance itself.

This work examines complementary frameworks for the governance of education that may favour democratic participation and a humanistic approach, while countering neo-liberal influences in the sector.

---

[6] Target 4.1 of Sustainable Development Goal 4. United Nations. 2015. *Transforming our World— The 2030 Agenda for Sustainable Development.*

[7] Verger, A., Lubienski, C. and Steiner-Khamsi, G. (Eds.) (2016). "The Emergence and Structuring of the Global Education Industry: Towards an Analytical Framework". In Verger, Lubienski and Steiner-Khamsi (eds.) *The Global Education Industry. World Yearbook of Education 2016.* London: Routledge.

1.3 Type of Research

The analysis conducted in this book is of theoretical nature. It builds on the work I carried out at United Nations Educational, Scientific and Cultural Organization (UNESCO) in Paris during my period of secondment at the Education Research and Foresight Unit (Education Sector). In particular, I had the privilege of providing research assistance in the realization of the report of the Senior Experts' Group established by the Director-General of UNESCO Irina Bokova to rethink education in a world of rapid transformation. The UNESCO flagship publication, *Rethinking Education: Towards a global common good?*, aims at revisiting foundational principles for the governance of education systems and at identifying issues likely to affect the organization of learning and the purposes of education in a context characterized by increasing complexity and uncertainty.

This research looks more deeply into the theoretical analysis developed in *Rethinking Education*, and in particular examines the need to revisit the concept of education as a public good in light of the trends of privatization and marketization which are increasingly affecting the educational landscape both at a national and at a global level.

It could be argued that this theoretical analysis falls within the category of what some scholars have called "research *of* policy" which is primarily characterized by critical analysis (Desjardins and Rubenson 2009). This type of research is distinct from the problem-solving approach which characterizes the so-called research *for* policy category, according to which the role of research is primarily directed at supporting decision-making and policy development by providing tools and solutions for policy action and design. The "research *of* policy" aims instead at clarifying concepts and principles, at providing a better understanding of issues which affect education policy, at expanding theories and thinking. As argued by Desjardins and Rubenson (2009), this more "conceptual position"

> developed as a criticism against the narrow interpretation of instrumentalism. The role of research is not primarily seen as coming up with a solution and/or answer to a specific issue but rather helps develop a broader understanding of the underlying problem. This involves widening the debate,

reformulating the problem, clarifying goals, and analyzing eventual conflicts between multiple goals. Instead of being of direct instrumental use, the primary function of research is conceptual. (2009: 13)

Indeed, if research *for* policy may be required to provide a concrete guide for action in order to respond to knowledge or action "gaps", it is also true that these gaps may occur because key concepts/principles may not be clear enough or should be revisited as they are no longer relevant to changing contexts. This requires another kind of research to be implemented: research *of* policy.

In order to provide a clearer understanding of the concept of public goods as applied to education, the work examines the economic theory of public goods and the way numerous scholars and experts have interpreted this notion, especially with regard to policy implications on the role and functions of the State. The analysis of education policy discourse is essential in order to highlight the conceptual frameworks and ideological underpinnings both of the actors that support a vision of education seen as a public good and of those who are more in favour of private involvement.

Through the analysis of discourse of the main actors involved in global education policy and the review of relevant literature, the study attempts to clarify the multifaceted phenomenon of privatization, considering administrative, economic, technical as well as political and social dimensions. This work also examines the extensive literature developed by several scholars and human rights researchers who caution against the potentially adverse impact that market approaches to education can have on equity and social justice. The review of the literature is grounded in an interdisciplinary perspective which examines political theory, economics, human rights law and philosophy as applied to the field of international education development. Moreover, the analysis of international education database and the review of research provide a detailed and systematic description of trends of private and market involvement in education.

Considering that the policies and issues related to marketization vary considerably at each level of education, this analysis will focus specifically on compulsory *schooling* since this is the level of education which receives most attention, partly "because it potentially affects the most people or involves the critical functions of education and socializing children" (Minow 2003: 1230). This is not to underestimate the significance of market mechanisms in early childhood, tertiary or higher education but to discuss all levels would exceed the scope of this work. Indeed, the privatization at each level of education displays itself in diverse ways, with different rationales and results. *Schooling* is also the level where the role of the State is more clearly established by international conventions and national laws. Moreover, this is the level which, over the last two decades, has been associated with global agendas such as Education for All and the Millennium Development Goals and on which the debates on privatization have focused the most.

1.4 Structure of the Book

Chapter 2, entitled "Different Interpretations of the Concept of Education As a Public Good in International Discourse", provides an analysis of education development discourse with regard to the use of the concept of education as a public good by the main actors involved in international education policy: UNESCO, UNICEF (United Nations Children's Fund), human rights treaty bodies, the Global Partnership for Education, the World Bank, the OECD (Organisation for Economic Co-operation and Development) and several international NGOs (non-governmental organizations). The analysis of policy documents, publications, reports and strategy papers is essential in order to highlight the conceptual frameworks, approaches and ideological underpinnings both of the actors that openly support a vision of education as a public good and of those who make no reference to this principle. It includes frame analysis techniques in order to determine the multiple, yet interrelated, conceptualizations of education as a public good by different international actors. These correspond respectively to an overall humanistic and integrated *vision of education* which is at the core of defining and preserving the collective interests of society (*policy focus*), which are the ultimate responsibility of the State (*principle of governance*). It is argued that these three interpretations represent three different closely interrelated facets of the same principle.

The purpose of the third chapter, entitled "Education: A Private or Public Good?", is to examine the extensive literature on the complex classification of public goods, which draws mainly on economic theories. It reviews existing research in the field of education and international development in order to highlight the way this concept has been applied to education and explores the limits of this transposition. Literature review on the application of the theory of public goods to the field of education seems inconclusive, as many authors have discussed the meaning and applicability of the concept of public good to education, often with contrasting visions and approaches. This chapter explores the extent to which education should be considered a public good. Ultimately, it critically examines the application of this concept at different levels, from basic to higher education, with reference to the extensive literature on the topic. This is necessary in order to determine the policy implications for the role of the State at the different levels of the education endeavour.

Chapter 4, entitled "A Changing Global Education Landscape: Growing Involvement of Non-State Actors", examines the multifaceted phenomenon of privatization through a review of education and development literature and considers its administrative, economic, technical, political and social dimensions. It identifies tensions related to the difficulty in finding a shared definition of privatization influenced by different disciplinary traditions which may have methodological implications when assessing the real scale of the phenomenon. This chapter provides a detailed and systematic description of how the involvement of non-state actors in education has been evolving since the 1990s in different regions worldwide, especially at the compulsory level. It further identifies some of the most significant rationales behind education privatization. In particular, it investigates one particular form of education privatization which is influenced by neo-liberal ideologies and market economics, providing an overview of the so-called Global Education Industry. The analysis examines the extensive literature developed by several scholars and human rights researchers cautioning against the potentially adverse impact that market approaches to education can have on equity and social justice, on democratic policy-making and governance, and on the societal/collective purposes of education. Considering the multifaceted process of privatization, and the greater involvement of economic actors

1 Introduction   11

in both the public and private domains, this chapter ends by suggesting that it is necessary to reframe the concept of education as a public good in the face of the blurring of boundaries between the public and the private.

The fifth chapter, entitled "Reframing the Concept of Education As a Public Good", first illustrates the peculiar nature of education, serving both public and private interests, and outlines two different approaches, one that puts greater emphasis on the public-goods and the other on private-goods aspects related to market-based approaches to education. The analysis provides insights into how the principle of education as a public good can be reinterpreted and outlines the policy implications with regard to the different functions of the State by taking into consideration different combinations of lower and higher levels of democracy and of private actors' involvement. It is argued that the State should maintain a fundamental regulatory function and should strengthen its role in the provision and funding of education, especially in those contexts where education systems are not fully developed. This chapter further identifies "criteria of publicness" that refer to both formal and functional conditions, the first related to the democratic governance of education systems and the latter to the development of democratic pedagogy and curriculum. It ultimately draws on the research by Gert Biesta (2012) who frames the theoretical debate on education in the public sphere.

Chapter 6, entitled "Education As a Common Good", examines complementary frameworks for the governance of education that may favour democratic participation and a humanistic approach while countering neo-liberal influences in the sector. Building on the concept of "the commons" as conceptualized by Elinor Ostrom, this book adopts a philosophical-political perspective on the notion of "common goods", considering it as a unitary category which goes beyond the economic classification of goods. It investigates the policy implications which result from the conceptualization of education as a common good in terms of humanistic vision, participatory democracy, community engagement and integrated approach to education. This framework implies a rethinking of political and economic paradigms and draws on recent studies of public policy and civil economy which may help identify more constructive and sustainable alternatives to address the challenges facing education systems

12   R. Locatelli

worldwide. It is argued that the frameworks of public goods and common goods may be seen as a continuum in line with the aim of strengthening the role of the State, not merely seen as a State consisting of separate individuals but as a "State-community" which identifies itself in the fulfilment of popular sovereignty.

Chapter 7, entitled "Going Global: Education As a Global Common Good", revisits normative principles for the global governance of education. It calls for the development of global political institutions that enable countries and their citizens to have greater voice in the decisions that affect their well-being. This is necessary to encourage the diversity of approaches while countering dominant development discourse, characterized by a more instrumental vision of education. This chapter discusses the extent to which the framework of global common goods may promote the formulation of democratic education policies and practices in a global context.

In conclusion, it is argued that there is a need to reframe education not only as a public but also as a common good. While greater public intervention and regulation are required in the field of education, it has also been suggested that it is necessary to significantly revisit and reshape the way public institutions themselves function in order to address the influence of the market in both the private and public domains. In the face of growing economic inequalities and of disruptive technological changes, it is necessary to reaffirm a humanistic approach to education while rebuilding an innovative sense of the community. The concept of education as a common good may contribute to the identification of participatory and democratic structures based on a vision of education seen not merely as an economic tool, but mainly as the process through which human beings and communities fully develop.

References

Apple, M., & Beane, J. A. (1995). *Democratic Schools*. Alexandria, VA: Association for Supervision and Curriculum Development.

Apple, M., & Beane, J. A. (2007). *Democratic Schools: Lessons in Powerful Education* (2nd ed.). Portsmouth, NH: Heinemann.

1 Introduction 13

Ball, S. J. (2007). *Education PLC*. London: Routledge.

Biesta, G. J. J. (2012). Becoming Public: Public Pedagogy, Citizenship and the Public Sphere. *Social & Cultural Geography, 13*(7), 683–697.

Desjardins, R., & Rubenson, K. (2009). *Research of vs Research for Education Policy—In an Era of Transnational Policy-Making*. Saarbrücken: VDM Verlag Dr.Müller.

Draxler, A. (2014). International Investment in Education for Development: Public Good or Economic Tool? In *Education, Learning, Training: Critical Issues for Development* (International Development Policy Series No. 5, Geneva: Graduate Institute Publications) (pp. 37–56). Boston: Brill-Nijhoff.

Hursh, D. W. (2016). *The End of Public Schools. The Corporate Reform Agenda to Privatize Education*. New York: Routledge.

Judt, T. (2010). *Ill Fares the Land*. New York: Penguin Books.

Kohlrausch, B., & Leuze, K. (2007). Implications of Marketization for the Perception of Education as Public or Private Good. In K. Martens, A. Rusconi, & K. Lutz (Eds.), *New Arenas of Education Governance* (pp. 195–213). New York: Palgrave Macmillan.

Labaree, D. F. (2011). Consuming the Public School. *Educational Theory, 61*(4), 381–394.

Levin, H. M. (2000). *The Public-Private Nexus in Education: Occasional Paper No. 1*. New York: National Center for the Study of Privatization in Education.

Macpherson, I., Robertson, S. L., & Walford, G. (Eds.). (2014). *Education, Privatization and Social Justice: Case Studies from Africa, South Asia and South East Asia*. Oxford: Symposium Books.

Mansbridge, J. (1998). On the Contested Nature of the Public Good. In W. Powell & E. Clemens (Eds.), *Private Action and the Public Good* (pp. 3–19). New Haven: Yale University Press.

Minow, M. (2003). Public and Private Partnerships: Accounting for the New Religion. *Harvard Law Review, 116*(5), 1229–1270.

Musgrave, R. A. (1959). *The Theory of Public Finance: A Study in Public Economy*. New York: McGraw-Hill Book Company.

Olson, M. (1965). *The Logic of Collective Action*. Cambridge, MA: Harvard University Press.

Reich, R. (2015). *Saving Capitalism: For the Many, Not the Few*. New York: Alfred Knopf.

Robertson, S. L., & Verger, A. (2012). Governing Education Through Public Private Partnerships. In S. L. Robertson, K. Mundy, A. Verger, & F. Menashy (Eds.), *Public Private Partnerships in Education: New Actors and Modes of Governance in a Globalizing World* (pp. 21–42). Cheltenham: Edward Elgar.

Robertson, S. L., Mundy, K., Verger, A., & Menashy, F. (2012). An Introduction to Public Private Partnerships and Education Governance. In S. L. Robertson, K. Mundy, A. Verger, & F. Menashy (Eds.), *Public Private Partnerships in Education: New Actors and Modes of Governance in a Globalizing World* (pp. 1–17). Cheltenham: Edward Elgar.

Samuelson, P. A. (1954). The Pure Theory of Public Expenditure. *The Review of Economics and Statistics, 36*(4), 387–389.

Tedesco, J. C. (1995). *The New Educational Pact: Education, Competitiveness and Citizenship in Modern Society.* Geneva: IBE-UNESCO.

UNESCO. (2015a). *Education 2030 Incheon Declaration and Framework for Action.* Paris: UNESCO.

UNESCO. (2015b). *World Education Forum 2015—Final Report.* Paris: UNESCO.

UNESCO. (2015c). *Rethinking Education: Towards a Global Common Good?* Paris: UNESCO.

UNESCO. (2016). *Education for People and Planet: Creating Sustainable Futures for All (Global Education Monitoring Report 2016).* Paris: UNESCO.

2

Different Interpretations of the Concept of Education As a Public Good in International Discourse

The conceptualization of education as a public good in development discourse is problematic. First and foremost, there are theoretical limitations inherent to the transposition of the economic concept of the public good to the field of education. This often leads to a lack of consensus regarding what the principle implies in terms of rights and responsibilities. Second, the conceptualization of education as a public good is now being challenged by the growing private involvement in education, as well as by the growing scale of for-profit education at all levels. Moreover, the principle of education as a public good, traditionally defined within the contours of the nation-state, is further challenged by the progressive shift in the locus of decision-making from the national to the global level. This blurring of boundaries between the public and the private and between the local and the global is undermining the relevance of the concept of education as a public good and as a guiding principle for democratic educational governance.

This chapter first looks at how the main actors involved in international education policy have referred to the concept of education as a public good and then examines the multiple, yet interrelated, levels of interpretation relating to this notion.

© The Author(s) 2019
R. Locatelli, *Reframing Education as a Public and Common Good*,
https://doi.org/10.1007/978-3-030-24801-7_2

15

2.1 Growing Reference to the Concept of Education As a Public Good Within International Education Development Discourse

This section provides an overview of the concept of education as a public good as understood by the main actors involved in international education development. The analysis of the most important policy documents—including in-house publications, policy reports and sector strategy papers—will be essential to determining the underlying ideological and conceptual frameworks on which these policies are based and to identifying which approaches and positions have been adopted when referring to this concept. With regard to the concept of discourse, in his book *Politics and policy making in education: Explorations in policy sociology*, Stephen Ball writes: "Discourses embody meaning and social relationships, they constitute both subjectivity and power relations […] the possibilities for meaning, for definition, are pre-empted through the social and institutional position from which a discourse comes" (1990: 17). The analysis carried out will therefore be essential in order to understand how and why these actors have been referring to the concept of education as a public good especially with regard to the role of the State in education policy and practice, since the time this notion was introduced into the language of international education and development.

Among the most significant actors are United Nations Educational, Scientific and Cultural Organization (UNESCO), which headed the global coordination of the Education for All agenda until 2015, and today leads the Education 2030 agenda as the United Nations' specialized agency for education, the Global Partnership for Education, as well as numerous international non-governmental organizations (NGOs) involved in education and development. Human rights actors have also been referring to the concept of education as a public good for some years. Although not explicitly envisaged in international human rights frameworks, the concept of education as a public good has been widely mentioned in numerous reports of the Special Rapporteurs on the Right to Education since 2000, as well as in several recommendations of the

2 Different Interpretations of the Concept of Education... 17

Human Rights Council (HRC), of the Committee on the Rights of the Child (CRC), and of the UN Committee on Economic, Social and Cultural Rights.

2.1.1 UNESCO and the International Coordination of the Education 2030 Agenda

The concept of education as a public good was first mentioned within the work of UNESCO during the 1990s to reaffirm a humanistic vision of education, based on principles of respect for life, human dignity, cultural diversity and social justice, in contrast to a more utilitarian and economic approach. The *Education for All* movement, which was first launched at the World Conference held in 1990 in Jomtien (Thailand), represented a milestone event which urged countries "to intensify efforts to address the basic learning needs of all"[1] and which reaffirmed the importance of education as a fundamental human right. The humanistic approach that underlay the *World Declaration on Education for All* was grounded on an integrated vision of education which, beyond economic factors, also considered "social, cultural, and ethical dimensions of human development" (UNESCO 1990). The importance of reaffirming an integrated and humanistic approach to education was in contrast with more utilitarian approaches which had been spreading worldwide since the 1970s as a result of neo-liberal policies and of the acceleration of economic globalization. Within the instrumentalist perspective of neo-liberalism, education is considered as one of the main drivers of economic development (Draxler 2014). It is in this context that in 1996, the International Commission on Education for the Twenty-first Century, chaired by Jacques Delors,[2] published the UNESCO landmark report *Learning: The Treasure Within*, commonly referred to as the *Delors Report*, in which it was affirmed that "education is a public good that should be available to all" (Delors et al. 1996). It has been argued that the humanistic and

---

[1] World Conference on EFA, Jomtien, 1990—retrieved at: www.unesco.org/new/en/education/themes/leading-the-international-agenda/education-for-all/the-efa-movement/jomtien-1990/.

[2] Jacques Delors is a French politician and economist who was president of the European Commission for three mandates between 1985 and 1995.

18   R. Locatelli

integrated vision of education conveyed in this report was based on a vision of "education as a public good with a fundamental role to play in personal and social development", one that should guide the mission of UNESCO as well as that of other UN agencies (Burnett 2008). As discussed by Tawil and Cougoureux (2013), this vision provided a guide for education systems in resistance to the "dominant utilitarian, economic tone prevalent at that time" (p. 4).

The notion of education as a public good has also been recalled in numerous documents produced essentially by UNESCO that contributed to the formulation of the post-2015 education agenda.[3] These documents underline that "the state is the custodian of quality education as a public good, recognizing the contribution of civil society, communities, families, learners and other stakeholders to education" (UNESCO 2014: 8).

In 2015, this principle was reaffirmed in the *Incheon Declaration on Education 2030*, which was adopted at the World Education Forum held in Incheon, Republic of Korea. It was also referred to as one of the core principles informing the *Framework for Action*. Under the statement "Education is a public good", the Framework for Action recalls the responsibility of the State as the main duty-bearer and its essential role in setting and regulating standards and norms, while also recognizing the role of all stakeholders in the realization of the right to quality education. The Framework for Action also includes a remark with regard to the involvement of the private sector in education financing, stating that it

---

[3] See in particular:

1. UNESCO, UNICEF. 2013. *Making Education a Priority in the Post-2015 Development Agenda*: Report of the Global Thematic Consultation on Education in the Post-2015 Development Agenda. UNESCO, UNICEF
2. UNESCO. 2013. *Thematic Consultation on Education in the post-2015 development agenda: Summary of Outcomes*. 18–19 March 2013 Dakar, Senegal
3. UNESCO's Executive Board at its 194th session, http://unesdoc.unesco.org/images/0022/002266/226628e.pdf
4. UNESCO. 2014. *Position Paper on Education Post-2015*. Paris, UNESCO February 2014, ED-14/EFA/POST-2015/1
5. UNESCO. 2014. *Joint Proposal of the EFA Steering Committee on Education Post-2015*. Paris, UNESCO. April 2014
6. UNESCO. 2014. *The Muscat Agreement*. Global Education for All Meeting. Muscat, Oman 12–14 May 2014, ED-14/EFA/ME/3
7. UNESCO. 2015. *Sharm El Sheikh Statement*. Arab States Regional Conference on Education Post-2015: Towards Quality Education and Lifelong Learning for All, Egypt 27–29 January 215

2 Different Interpretations of the Concept of Education... 19

"will be essential to ensure that spending on education from the private sector is oriented [...] to reinforce education as a public good".[4] It is therefore evident that UNESCO, as leading the coordination of the Sustainable Development Goal (SDG) 4—*Ensure inclusive and equitable quality education and promote lifelong learning opportunities for all*—considers the concept of education as a public good a key feature of the renewed global Education 2030 agenda. The importance of reaffirming this principle is also dependent on the need to identify and develop "new ways to increase public education budgets through greater fiscal capacity, innovative partnerships with non-state actors, as well as through advocacy for increased official development assistance" (UNESCO 2016: 3).

Since 2015, the principle of education as a public good has been widely mentioned in the policy reports and outcome statements of regional meetings which have been presented in the framework of the Education 2030 global and regional coordination mechanisms set out by UNESCO. At the opening session of its 4th Meeting, the SDG-Education 2030 Steering Committee highlighted "a renewed commitment to investment in education, which should be based on the fundamental principles of education as a human right, a public good, and a collective responsibility" (UNESCO 2018a: 1). With reference to the increasing efforts to address the financing challenges and to fill the financing gap and achieve SDG4, the Steering Committee recommended that "All financing initiatives respect the principle of education as fundamental human right and a public good of which the State is the duty bearer" (UNESCO 2018b: 2). Reference to the promotion of education as a public good and a public responsibility, or in the public interest, was also made during the African, Arab, European and North American regional meetings.[5] Moreover, the outcome document of the Global Education Meeting held in Brussels in December 2018 to review the SDG4-Education 2030 agenda with regard to progress made also stressed the importance of "improving the accountability of education as a public good" and reaffirmed "that education is a public good and public responsibility" (UNESCO 2018c: 1).

---

[4] UNESCO. 2015a. *Education 2030 Incheon Declaration and Framework for Action*. Paris, UNESCO. http://unesdoc.unesco.org/images/0024/002432/243278e.pdf.

[5] Outcome Statements of Regional Education 2030 Consultations are available at this link: https://en.unesco.org/themes/education/globaleducationmeeting2018.

UNESCO and Higher Education As a Public Good

Although this work mainly focuses on basic levels of education, it is important to acknowledge that the concept of education as a public good also represents a fundamental principle for discussions that have been held regarding other levels of education, especially higher education. The participants in the UNESCO 2009 World Conference on Higher Education recognized higher education as a public good. Indeed, in the Final Communiqué (UNESCO 2009), they supported the idea that, as a public good, higher education should be the responsibility not only of governments but also of society at large (§1). With particular regard to issues of funding, it is stated that "Education remains a public good, but private financing should be encouraged. While every effort must be made to increase public funding of higher education, it must be recognised that public funds are limited and may not be sufficient for such a rapidly developing sector. Other formulae and sources of funding, especially those drawing on the public-private partnership model, should be found" (§47). It could be argued that discussions on the concept of public goods as applied to higher education have mainly centred on issues of funding and on the function of higher education institutions, rather than on questions of delivery and ownership. Forms of state funding and regulation have been considered as necessary to ensure equitable and affordable higher education opportunities, especially when considering the striking inequalities that affect higher education systems worldwide (UNESCO and UNESCO IIEP 2017; Marginson 2016).

2.1.2 Human Rights Discourse

Within human rights discourse, the notion of education as a public good was considered by Katarina Tomaševski, the first UN Special Rapporteur on the Right to Education, as the premise of any "governmental human rights obligations".[6] One of the interesting features of her reports regards

---

[6] Report submitted by the Special Rapporteur, Katarina Tomaševski, on the right to education. E/CN.4/2004/45, 15 January 2004. See also other reports: E/CN.4/2000/6, 1; E/CN.4/2001/52, 11; E/CN.4/2004/45, 15.

2 Different Interpretations of the Concept of Education... 21

the distinction that she made about the concept of *education* as a public good and of *schooling* as a public service:

> The Special Rapporteur deems that education constitutes a public good because its worth increases when it is shared and it cannot be prevented from spreading. Different from education, schooling cannot easily be defined as a public good because individuals can be prevented from having access to school. The denial of formal schooling cannot be equated with a lack of education—people learn at home, on the street, in the community, in prison or refugee camps. (Tomaševski 2001: 21)

The affirmation of this principle aimed at warning against the greater influence of economic discourse and the prospects of education being considered as a commodity and reduced to a means for creating human capital. The changing status of education was considered the result of the greater importance attributed to economic principles of consumer choice, competitiveness and international trade in education services. Hence, the need to reaffirm the role of the State as a "powerful antidote against the risk of depleting education of remaining a public good and schooling from remaining a public service" (Tomaševski 2001: 9).

More recent reports transmitted to the UN Human Rights Council and to the General Assembly by Kishore Singh, Special Rapporteur on the Right to Education between the years 2010 and 2016, also highlight the primary responsibility of the State in expanding public education opportunities and public investment against the risk of commercialization and "mercantalization of education".[7] Moreover, the formulation of a "Regulatory framework for governing private providers, centered on education as a public good" is considered of critical importance in establishing responsibilities and accountability requirements. The UN Special Rapporteur also argued that "regulations must ensure that education is accessible to all, works towards the broader public interest and reflects a broad humanistic notion of education".[8] Together with the principle of

---

[7] Report of the UN Special Rapporteur Kishore Singh on the right to education. *Privatization and the right to education.* A/69/402, 24 September 2014. See also: *Report on the Post-2015 Education Agenda.* A/68/294, 09 August 2013.

[8] Report of the UN Special Rapporteur Kishore Singh on the right to education. *Protecting the right to education against commercialization.* A/HRC/29/30, 10 June 2015, §94.

22   R. Locatelli

education as a human right, which compels States to respect, protect and fulfil the right to education,[9] the notion of education as a public good is clearly pointed out by the UN Special Rapporteur in order to counterbalance potential harmful effects of the involvement of non-state actors in the sector, since principles of equity, equality and non-discrimination could be undermined. In this perspective, the State is expected to directly fund, provide and regulate education opportunities. The UN Special Rapporteur on the right to education constantly emphasized the importance of "safeguarding education as a public good", and this position was reiterated also in the report on the issue of public–private partnerships.[10]

Partly as a result of the number of reports regarding the impact of privatization on the right to education presented to UN human rights treaty bodies by civil society organizations,[11] the Human Rights Council (HRC) and the Committee on the Rights of the Child (CRC) both raised issues about the growing involvement of private, for-profit actors in the sector and recommended that all actors should "contribute to education as a public good".[12] For instance, in a report presented at the UN General Assembly on 29 June 2016, the Human Rights Council urged

> all States to expand educational opportunities for all without discrimination, recognizing the significant importance of investment in public education to the maximum of available resources, to increase and improve domestic and external financing for education as affirmed in the Incheon Declaration and the Education 2030 Framework for Action, to ensure that education policies and programmes are consistent with human rights standards and principles, including those laid down in the Universal Declaration of Human Rights and in relevant international human rights instruments, and to strengthen engagement with all relevant stakeholders, including

---

[9] CESCR, General Comment N. 13 on the Right to Education (Article 13 of the Covenant), 21st session, 08/12/1999, E/C.12/1999/10, §46.

[10] Report of the UN Special Rapporteur Kishore Singh on the right to education. A/70/342, 26 August 2015.

[11] These civil society organizations include, above all, the Right to Education Project, the Global Initiative for Economic, Social and Cultural Rights, Education International as well as numerous country-based civil society organizations. The full list of UN treaty bodies' resolutions and reports is available at this link: http://globalinitiative-escr.org/advocacy/privatization-in-education-research-initiative.

[12] UN Human Rights Council Resolution. 2015. The Right to Education. A/HRC/RES/29/7, 22 July 2015.

2 Different Interpretations of the Concept of Education... 23

communities, local actors and civil society, to contribute to education as a public good.[13]

2.1.3 Civil Society Organizations and NGOs

As aforementioned, the notion of education as a public good has also been mentioned by several civil society organizations involved in education development. The non-governmental organizations taking part in the NGO Forum at the World Education Forum (Republic of Korea—May 2015) referred to this notion in order to "reject calls for increased privatisation or commercialisation in education, including any support for low fee private schools and for-profit universities" (UNESCO and CCNGO 2015: 14g). Among the many international civil society organizations and NGOs, the Right to Education Initiative and the Global Initiative for Economic, Social and Cultural Rights have been playing a primary role in supporting public education systems according to human rights frameworks. They were also some of the key promoters of the consultative process which, in February 2019, led to the adoption of the *Abidjan Principles on the human rights obligations of States to provide public education and to regulate private involvement in education.*[14] These organizations have always promoted a vision of education as a public good, especially considering the recent involvement of for-profit actors in education worldwide. Given some critiques that have been moved on the validity of the principle of public good as applied to education,[15] in more recent years, their discourse slightly changed in favour of considering education as a public *service*, deeming that this notion would make it even clearer that education, especially at the compulsory level, is a responsibility of the State that has to directly deliver, fund and regulate education systems.

Education International (EI), the global teachers' unions organization, recalls the notion of "education as a public good" in its discourse, underlining how important it is that "the costs of public education should [...]

---

[13] Human Rights Council. *The right to education.* A/HRC/32/L.33, 29 June 2016, §3.

[14] The Abidjan Principles are available at the following link: https://www.abidjanprinciples.org/.

[15] See below UNESCO (2015) and Daviet (2016).

24   R. Locatelli

not be disproportionately borne by poorer citizens"[16] and advocating against the risks of transforming education from a public good into a commodity which would give more importance to private profit rather than to educational principles and student learning.[17] With public education under unprecedented threat, the EI's 7th World Congress held in 2015 resolved to continue their "Unite for Quality Education" by demonstrating that privatization undermines public education and is detrimental to the interests of society. Thus, EI's *Global Response to the Commercialisation and Privatisation of Education* was born where the growing privatization and commercialization of education is challenged as "one of the greatest threats to education as a human right and a public good and [to] the achievement of *SDG4: inclusive and equitable, free quality education for all*".[18]

The Global Campaign for Education (GCE), known as "the world's biggest civil society movement working to end the global education crisis" (GCE 2016), also considers the concept of education as a public good and a guiding principle for any action taken in the sector. In this regard, the GCE supports the idea that the State has the primary responsibility of financing, providing and regulating education in order to overcome inequalities and injustice. In 2017, the GCE elaborated a toolkit entitled *Public Good over Private Profit: A Toolkit for Civil Society to Resist the Privatisation of Education* intended as a resource for civil society coalitions and organizations who want to have a better understanding of the development and impact of privatization in the education sector in their country (GCE 2017).

2.1.4   International Bodies and Organizations

Among the international organizations with a stake in education and development, the Global Partnership for Education, formerly known as the *Education for All—Fast Track Initiative*, also envisages the concept of

---

[16] *Education For All and The Global Development Agenda Beyond 2015: Principles For A Post-2015 Education And Development Framework*. Bruxelles, Education International.

[17] Privatisation: https://ei-ie.org/en/detail_page/4654/privatisation.

[18] A global response to commercialisation of education: https://www.unite4education.org/about/a-global-response-to-education-commercialisation/.

2 Different Interpretations of the Concept of Education... 25

"Education as a public good" as the first principle listed in its *Strategic Plan 2016–2020* which acts as a guide for the work of the organization (GPE 2016). With a specific focus on supporting the development of public education systems in developing countries, the Global Partnership for Education enhances public financial capacities of both recipient countries as well as of donors through contributions to the partnership. The concept of education as a public good can be interpreted as a call for greater consolidation of public education systems through public funding.

Reference to this concept is also present in the policy documents and reports produced by the Organisation for Economic Co-operation and Development (OECD). Attention, however, should be paid to the way this notion is being used. In the Review of OECD education policies, it is stated that "Primary, secondary and post-secondary non-tertiary education is usually conceived of as a public good and is mainly financed by public funds."[19] By using the expression "is usually conceived", it could be argued that the way this statement is framed is meant to reflect the major considerations regarding the funding of national education systems of the States which are part of the organization rather than the perspective on this theme of the organization itself. In the 2014 and 2015 *Education at a Glance* reports, this statement is recalled basically to highlight an important policy issue regarding the way different levels of education should be funded. While the question of funding to tertiary education is still being widely debated, it is acknowledged that compulsory education "is usually conceived as a public good and is thus largely financed by public funds" (OECD 2015, 2014). Mention of this term is however lacking in the following 2016, 2017 and 2018 *Education at a Glance* reports.

Moreover, in the World Bank's discourse, there are no references to this concept. On the contrary, in a 2014 a blog post by Shanta Devarajan[20] entitled *Education as if Economics Mattered*, it is stated (perhaps provocatively) that education mainly constitutes a "private good" because of the individual benefits it produces. This was seen as one of the main reasons

---

[19] OECD Review Education Policies website: http://gpseducation.oecd.org/revieweducationpolicies/#!node=41707&filter=all.

[20] Shanta Devarajan is currently the Senior Director for Development Economics (DEC) and the acting Chief Economist for the World Bank Group.

26   R. Locatelli

why people are turning to private markets and for the failure of public education systems.[21] This blog caused an immediate reaction among researchers and civil society organizations, and the publication of a blog post by Steve Klees[22] entitled *Education as if People Mattered* in response to the World Bank blog, where the author advocated for the public-good dimensions of education.[23]

2.2   Diverse Levels of Interpretation

As illustrated so far, the notion of education as a public good has been increasingly mentioned in international education development discourse since the 1990s, although with different interpretations and purposes. The use and frequency of the concept of education as a public good in reports and policy documents can denote the underlying ideological and conceptual frameworks informing the policies and it can help identify which approaches and visions of education these actors have been adopting. For instance, reference to this notion in the discourse of the World Bank and of the OECD is either omitted or very weak. This may reflect an approach to education grounded in human capital or economic instrumentalism (Menashy 2013).

By contrast, this notion has been recalled by international actors, such as UNESCO, human rights treaty bodies and civil society organizations, whose mission is clearly grounded on a human rights framework and whose main concerns are related to principles of equity, social justice and non-discrimination in education: First and foremost, it has been used to reaffirm a humanistic and integrated *vision of education* which goes beyond narrow utilitarian economic approaches. This was clearly the concern expressed both by the UNESCO Delors Commission in 1996 and by the first UN Special Rapporteur on the Right to Education in

---

[21] Education as if Economics Mattered: http://blogs.worldbank.org/futuredevelopment/education-if-economics-mattered.

[22] Steve Klees is Professor of International Education at the College of Education, University of Maryland.

[23] Education as if People Mattered: https://worldsofeducation.org/en/woe_homepage/woe_detail/4788/education-as-if-people-mattered.

2 Different Interpretations of the Concept of Education... 27

2000. In addition, the notion of education as a public good has been adopted as a *policy focus*, to underlie the public interest and enhance social development, in contrast to a limited focus on individual private benefits. This facet can be related to the instrumental role of education in producing positive societal externalities such as increasing social cohesion and shared values as well as a country's economic growth, innovation capacity and competitiveness (Daviet 2016). Finally, it has been referred to as a *principle of governance* to suggest the need to strengthen the functions and role of the State in a context characterized by the growing involvement of non-state actors in educational policy and provision. This can be related to the need to make education non-excludable and non-rivalrous, according to the very characteristics of public goods in the strict economic sense. Given its intrinsic value, education should be available to all. This is strictly associated to the need to reinforce the responsibility of public authorities in respecting and fulfilling this principle, which requires them to ensure public funds and provision.

The diverse interpretations of the principle of education as a public good in education development discourse appear, therefore, highly interrelated. Whether interpreted as an approach/vision, as a policy focus or as a principle of governance, the principle of education as a public good refers to the definition and preservation of collective interests of society and to the central responsibility of the State in doing so. These different interpretations can be synthetized in Table 2.1.

Although these three different interpretations represent closely interrelated facets of the same principle, for the purposes of this analysis, particular attention will be paid to the conceptualization of education as a public good as a *principle of governance*. Indeed, the focus on education governance may provide insight into how this principle influences the way policies, priorities, resources and reforms are managed and implemented and how power relations at different levels are distributed.

However, despite the growing reference to this notion in education development discourse since the 1990s, and even more so since 2000, questions have been raised regarding the applicability of the economic theory of public goods to the field of education (UNESCO 2015; Daviet 2016). The 2015 UNESCO publication *Rethinking Education: Towards a*

28   R. Locatelli

Table 2.1 Levels of interpretation of the concept of education as a public good in education development discourse

As an approach/vision	To reaffirm a humanistic/integrated vision of education in contrast to a more utilitarian approach
As a policy focus	To preserve the public interest and societal/collective development in contrast to an individualistic perspective
As a principle of governance	To reaffirm the role of the State as the guarantor/custodian/main duty-bearer of education in light of the greater involvement of non-state actors at all levels of the education endeavour

global common good?[24] affirmed the need to re-contextualize the concept of education as a public good in the light of the changing educational global landscape. In this report, some issues were raised with regard to the applicability of the concept of public goods to the field of education and to the limits of this normative principle for educational governance, especially regarding the ability of the State to directly fund, provide and regulate education opportunities. This was based on the greater acknowledgement that the role of the State is increasingly being challenged by growing involvement of non-state actors, which call into question the very nature of what is considered as "public" in education. Moreover, it was stated "there is no general agreement, in much of the discussion, about [its] applicability to post-basic education and training" and to non-formal education in general (UNESCO 2015: 11).

The principle of education as a public good has also been deemed ineffective to counter the consequences of privatization and commodification. According to Daviet (2016), the economic underpinnings of the theory of public goods, grounded in neoclassical economic theory, "conflict with the principles underlying the humanistic approach to education" (p. 5). It may therefore follow that the concept of education as a public good, which has been adopted by international governmental and non-governmental organizations to counterbalance distortive effects of the market in education, may in reality promote greater privatization and

---

[24] This report sought to update and build on the Delors Report and served as a normative reference for the vision and principles outlined in the Education 2030 Framework for Action.

2 Different Interpretations of the Concept of Education... 29

a more utilitarian/economic approach. Having said this, even though the concept of education as a public good does not comply completely with the standard definition of a *pure* public good—being it completed "with ethical considerations that are foreign to it or complement its core line of thought with other economic theories" (Daviet 2016)—it does imply in any case some sort of intervention on the part of the State. Education can be considered as an "impure" public good which generates positive externalities and positive effects on equity and social justice. In this perspective, some form of state intervention is required. Therefore, it seems unlikely that the use of this concept would foster privatization and marketization. On the contrary, the fact that some international aid agencies with clear neo-liberal ideological underpinnings, such as the World Bank, do not refer to this concept in their discourse shows that they may be unwilling to consider a strong intervention of the State in the field of education as necessary.

Since processes of privatization increasingly promote education as a tradable commodity, a shift towards the perception of education as a private good seems likely (Kohlrausch and Leuze 2007). The following section explores the economic theory of public goods and its applicability to the field of education. It analyses different interpretations that many scholars have given to this notion, particularly with regard to the role of the State at different levels. Determining whether the notion of education as a public good is still valid and relevant for education policy has become all the more important in recent years as growing trends of education privatization may lead to the risk of considering education as a mere private or marketable/consumable good. Indeed, when there is a need to state the obvious, it is often an indication that it is no longer the case (Bergan et al. 2009).

References

Ball, S. (1990). *Politics and Policy Making in Education: Explorations in Policy Sociology*. London: Routledge.

Bergan, S., Guarga, R., Egron Polak, F., Dias Sobrinho, J., Tandon, R., & Tilak, J. B. G. (2009). Public Responsibility for Higher Education. *2009 World Conference on Higher Education*. Paris: UNESCO.

30   R. Locatelli

Burnett, N. (2008). The Delors Report: A Guide Towards Education for All. *European Journal of Education, 43*(2), 181–187.

Daviet, B. (2016). *Revisiting the Principle of Education as a Public Good.* ERF Working Papers No. 17. Paris: UNESCO Education Research and Foresight.

Delors, et al. (1996). *Learning: The Treasure Within. Report to UNESCO of the International Commission on Education for the Twenty-first Century.* Paris: UNESCO.

Draxler, A. (2014). International Investment in Education for Development: Public Good or Economic Tool? In *Education, Learning, Training: Critical Issues for Development* (pp. 37–56). International Development Policy series No. 5. Geneva and Boston: Graduate Institute Publications and Brill-Nijhoff.

GCE. (2016). *Private Profit Public Loss: Why the Push for Low-Fee Private Schools Is Throwing Quality Education off Track.* Johannesburg: Global Campaign for Education.

GCE. (2017). *Public Good Over Private Profit: Toolkit for Civil Society to Resist the Privatisation of Education.* Johannesburg: Global Campaign for Education. Retrieved from https://www.campaignforeducation.org/wp/wp-content/uploads/2018/04/Public_Good_Over_Private_Profit_TOOLKIT_EN.pdf.

GPE. (2016). *Strategic Plan 2016–2020.* Washington, DC: Global Partnership for Education.

Kohlrausch, B., & Leuze, K. (2007). Implications of Marketization for the Perception of Education as Public or Private Good. In K. Martens, A. Rusconi, & K. Lutz (Eds.), *New Arenas of Education Governance* (pp. 195–213). New York: Palgrave Macmillan.

Marginson, S. (2016). Public/Private in Higher Education: A Synthesis of Economic and Political Approaches. *Studies in Higher Education, 43*(2), 322–337.

Menashy, F. (2013). Interrogating an Omission: The Absence of a Rights-based Approach to Education in World Bank Policy Discourse. *Discourse: Studies in the Cultural Politics of Education, 34*(5), 749–764. https://doi.org/10.1080/0 1596306.2013.728368.

OECD. (2014). *Education at a Glance 2014: OECD Indicators.* OECD Publishing.

OECD. (2015). *Education at a Glance 2015: OECD Indicators.* OECD Publishing.

Tawil, S., & Cougoureux, M. (2013). *Revisiting Learning: The Treasure Within— Assessing the Influence of the 1996 Delors Report.* ERF Occasional Papers No. 4. Paris: UNESCO Education Research and Foresight.

2 Different Interpretations of the Concept of Education... 31

Tomaševski, L. (2001). *Human Rights Obligations: Making Education Available, Accessible, Acceptable and Adaptable*. Right to Education Primers No. 3.

UNESCO. (1990, March 5–9). *World Declaration on Education for All and Framework for Action to Meet Basic Learning Needs*. Adopted by the World Conference on Education for All "Meeting Basic Learning Needs" (Jomtien, Thailand). Paris: UNESCO.

UNESCO. (2009). *Communiqué—2009 World Conference on Higher Education: The New Dynamics of Higher Education and Research For Societal Change and Development*. Paris: UNESCO.

UNESCO. (2014, May 12–14). *The Muscat Agreement*. Global Education for All Meeting. Muscat, Oman, ED-14/EFA/ME/3.

UNESCO. (2015). *Rethinking Education: Towards a Global Common Good?* Paris: UNESCO.

UNESCO. (2016). *Unpacking SDG 4—Education 2030 Commitments: Education 2030—Briefing Note 2: Key Features and commitments*. Paris: UNESCO.

UNESCO. (2018a, February 28–March 2). *Meeting Report*. 4th Meeting of the SDG-Education 2030 Steering Committee, Paris. Paris: UNESCO. Retrieved from https://unesdoc.unesco.org/ark:/48223/pf0000261973.

UNESCO. (2018b, February 28–March 2). *Synthesis of Key Recommendations and Decisions*. SDG-Education 2030 Steering Committee, Paris. Paris: UNESCO. Retrieved from https://en.unesco.org/sites/default/files/sdg-ed_2030_steering_committee_-_recommendations_and_decisions_-_8_march_2018_final_0.pdf.

UNESCO. (2018c, December 3–5). *Brussels Declaration*. Global Education Meeting 2018, Brussels. Paris: UNESCO.

UNESCO & UNESCO IIEP. (2017, April). *Six Ways to Ensure Higher Education Leaves no One Behind*. Policy Paper No. 30. Paris: UNESCO.

UNESCO and CCNGO. (2015, May). *Towards the Right to Inclusive Quality Public Education and Lifelong Learning Beyond 2015*. NGO Declaration, World Education Forum—Incheon, Republic of Korea—ED/WEF2015/NGO/3.

3

Education: A Private or Public Good?

An appropriate analysis of the concept of education as a public good, and of the implications with regard to the role of the State in the governance of education systems, requires a preliminary overview of the traditional theory of public goods. First of all, how has the concept of public goods been defined in economic theory? What does it imply for the role of the State in terms of functions and responsibilities? How has the notion of education as a public good been interpreted in education research? What are the implications for the role of the State at different levels of education? This chapter examines the concept of public goods as conceptualized in economic theory and highlights the potential limits and challenges of its transposition to the field of education.

3.1 The Transposition of the Theory of Public Goods to Education

The notion of public goods has always been linked to the functions and role of the State in modern, Western societies. The concept of "public goods" is rooted in the culture of the eighteenth century and

© The Author(s) 2019
R. Locatelli, *Reframing Education as a Public and Common Good*,
https://doi.org/10.1007/978-3-030-24801-7_3

34   R. Locatelli

can be traced back to classical economics. In his *Treatise of Human Nature*, published for the first time in 1739, the philosopher David Hume was one of the first to analyse the difficulties concerning the provision of "public goods". About 30 years later, Adam Smith explored this subject in his *Inquiry into the Nature and Causes of the Wealth of Nations* (1776). Hume and Smith both "agreed that government intervention is needed to supply goods and services characterized by collective benefits. If left to the spontaneous action of individuals or organizations, these goods would not be adequately provided" (Razzolini 2004: 457).

3.1.1   The Economic Theory of Public Goods

Following a major contribution by Richard Musgrave in 1939, a modern and complete theory on public goods was developed for the first time by Paul Samuelson in 1954 with the publication of his foundational paper *The Pure Theory of Public Expenditure*. Samuelson is considered the first economist to propose a theory of public goods in a welfare-state context (Andersen and Lindsnaes 2007). In his work, he defined public goods as "*collective consumption goods* [...] which all enjoy in common in the sense that each individual's consumption of such a good leads to no subtraction from any other individual's consumption of that good" (p. 387). This is the property that has become known as "non-rivalry".

In addition, public goods exhibit a second property called "non-excludability" whereby it is impossible to exclude any individuals from consuming the good. This second characteristic was not mentioned by Samuelson in his work of 1954. Musgrave's second technical characteristic of a public good, non-excludability, is implicitly added in Samuelson's 1958 paper. In a strictly economic sense, therefore, a public good has two distinguishing properties: one person's consumption does not preclude another's (non-rivalry) and to exclude anyone from consumption is costly, if not impossible (non-excludability). Examples of public goods include clean air, lighthouses and national security: these goods fulfil the characteristics of non-rivalry and non-excludability since it is difficult—and costly—

3 Education: A Private or Public Good?   35

to exclude someone benefitting from them (non-excludability) and since no one's use detracts from that of others (non-rivalry).

Goods with these two characteristics present several problems for the free market, one of which is the *free-rider* problem. According to classical economic theory, in the case of public goods, individuals tend to act as "free riders", a phenomenon occurring when people make use of the advantages of the non-exclusion situation where they do not pay for the use of goods that have already been paid for (Buchanan 1975). In this situation, the free market does not have the possibility of linking the enjoyment and consumption of a good with payment for its provision or its production, and it is unprofitable for markets to make these goods available free of charge. Therefore, if people do not pay for the enjoyment of public goods, less will be invested in such goods than is optimal. In a free market system, public goods will be underprovided (Ver Eecke 2008: 64). Since the competitive market may fail to guarantee the optimal provision of goods with these characteristics and price them efficiently, public goods are considered as *market failures*, requiring some forms of intervention by the State (Ver Eecke 2008; Marginson 2007). It should be noted that, in market-based economies, public goods have always been considered a category residual to that of private goods, "exceptions to the idea of private goods" (Ver Eecke 2008: 6). Indeed, Western economic thinking has always given priority to the concept of private goods, because this is directly connected to the wishes of consumers.

The classical definition, therefore, highlights the market-state issue: the provision of private goods is assigned to the market and of public goods to the State (Kaul and Mendoza 2003). However, the analytical understanding of public goods has expanded since the 1950s giving rise to different interpretations among economists. This has led to the multiplication of categories of public goods which differentiate between *pure* public goods, which possess the two characteristics of non-rivalry and non-excludability, and *impure* public goods, such as common pool resources or club goods, which possess the two characteristics in different measures (Cornes and Sandler 1986) (Table 3.1).

36 R. Locatelli

Table 3.1 Private and public goods

	Rivalrous	Non-rivalrous
Excludable	Private good	Network Club good (mostly non-rivalrous inside the club)
Non-excludable	Good subject to congestion or depletion, yet accessible to all Some global commons (geostationary orbit)	Pure public good Existence value Some global commons (high seas, ozone layer)

Source: Kaul et al. (1999)
Note: Public goods are in the shaded areas

3.1.2 Beyond Economic Theory, to Socio-political Considerations

Discussion on the role of the State in the financing and in the provision of public goods, including education, is inevitably influenced by the complex classification of public goods and by the lack of consensus among economists in determining their nature (Malkin and Wildavsky 1991; Adams and McCormick 1993; Cornes and Sandler 1994; Kaul and Mendoza 2003). It should be noted that at the time when the concept of public goods was conceptualized in the mid-1950s, "economists and the world at large favored an active role for the state in the economy" and therefore in the provision of public goods (Desai 2003: 65). However, some have deemed that the concept of public goods does not imply a direct involvement of the State. Indeed, some authors have argued that public goods are nothing but a *social construct* for there are different definitions of the concept, and different countries treat different services as public goods. As clearly stated, "they are public because and only because society chooses to put the goods in the public sector instead of the private sector" (Malkin and Wildavsky 1991: 355).

3 Education: A Private or Public Good? 37

In this respect, it may appear that there are no objective criteria in defining public goods and that technical or inherent characteristics do not justify an intervention of the State which cannot be counted on to optimally provide a public good, since "there may be governmental failure as well as market failure, and governmental failure may be worse than market failure" (Malkin and Wildavsky 1991: 371). Considerations on methods of taxation, financing and provision of education appear to be grounded on the diverse interpretations given to the theory of public goods. If we assume that public goods are such only because they reflect a social construct, the financing and delivery of educational opportunities will be left to the choices of the political parties that decide whether to pay, or not to pay, for the provision of a determined good.

In his book *The Ethical Dimensions of the Economy*, Wilfried Ver Eecke[1] provides a helpful contribution to address the challenges relating to the uncertainty regarding the role of the State in the provision of public goods. Indeed, he argues that "the concept of 'public good' is a valid, even though problematic, concept for analyzing certain economic problems" (2008: 145). While acknowledging the claim that the State cannot always be considered as the optimal provider of public goods (Malkin and Wildavsky 1991) and that private initiatives can also provide some public goods (Olson 1965), Ver Eecke demonstrates the validity of the technical characteristics of public goods and objects to the idea that the concept of "public good" is merely a *social construct*. In his view, this notion "has a clearly defined ideal content [which] is empirically present only in varying degrees and has no agreed upon implementation strategy" (Ver Eecke 2008: 145). The concepts of public and private good are therefore concepts that cannot be found in reality. Indeed, in real life, economic events are more or less public goods rather than strictly *pure* public goods (Ver Eecke 2008). Therefore, the question to ask is which aspects of a particular good exhibit the characteristics typical of the concept of private or public good. Ver Eecke reviews the thorough classification of goods to demonstrate that the categories of public, private and merit good are sufficient to describe different phenomena of reality—in his opinion, any additional adjective would be superfluous.

---

[1] Wilfried Ver Eecke is Professor of philosophy at Georgetown University in Washington, DC.

It is therefore acknowledged that the State has some duties and responsibilities with regard to the provision of public goods. Indeed, while the problem of public goods represents a pure economic challenge—since there are no optimal economic solutions—non-economic factors may play an important role in the choice of solutions to the problem of public goods. Samuelson and Olson—who addressed the two characteristics of public goods—also concluded that a general optimal economic solution to this problem does not exist. The discussion on public goods therefore requires "ethical and political judgments" and a broader reflection on social and institutional arrangements which do not diminish the validity of the concept of public good itself (Ver Eecke 2008).

3.2 Is Education a Public Good?

Many experts have debated on the meaning and applicability of the concept of public good to education, often with contrasting visions and approaches. The analysis of this theme can be organized around two key steps which may help to clarify this discussion. First of all, it is important to establish whether some intervention on the side of the State is to be expected, and therefore to determine whether education can fall within the classification of public goods. Moreover, once agreed whether education can be considered as a public good, requiring State intervention, it is important to understand what the nature of that intervention should be.

3.2.1 Which Justifications for State Intervention?

Determining whether or not education is a public good (be it impure, mixed or by design) is related to considerations about the existence of conditions for state intervention.

According to a narrow interpretation of the economic theory of public goods, education may appear as a *private* good. Indeed, education does not correspond to the classical definition of a *pure public good*, that is, a good that has both characteristics of non-excludability and non-rivalry. For example, classroom space can be excludable and a higher number of

3 Education: A Private or Public Good? 39

students in a class may affect the quality of education being provided and consumed, making it rivalrous (Menashy 2009). It follows that if education were a private good, control would be left to individuals acting through market mechanisms. According to Shanta Devarajan, Senior Director for Development Economics at the World Bank, education is "largely a private good" since most of the benefits accrue to the individual. In his opinion, education should be provided and funded by the private sector like any other market, with the State merely providing the regulatory framework for private involvement.[2] Others have considered education as a "merit good", one which has the characteristics of both a private and a public good (Musgrave 1959). In economic theory, a merit good is defined by Musgrave as a good which is so important that when the competent authorities are dissatisfied with the level of consumption in the free market, they can intervene, even against the wishes of consumers (1959). Therefore, the provision on the side of the State of some goods such as education is based on ethical/value judgements. The uncertainty regarding the classification of education according to economic theory inevitably results in uncertainty concerning the role and the functions of the State in education at different levels, from policy-making, to funding, provision, regulation and monitoring.

Despite the economic characteristics of education as an excludable and rivalrous good, in most countries it has been turned into a free, universally available and compulsory service provided by the State, thereby exhibiting the characteristics of non-rivalry and non-excludability typical of public goods (Menashy 2009). Those who consider education as being an *impure* public good, or a public good *by design*, acknowledge the fact that it can be somehow excludable and rivalrous, but nevertheless justify state intervention on the basis of other economic considerations, mainly related to the public benefits that education engenders, such as overcoming inequality among individuals. These collective benefits include a country's economic growth, innovation capacity and competitiveness, social cohesion and shared values (Daviet 2016). Private supply does not guarantee the attainment of the level of production that maximizes collective well-being.

---

[2] Devarajan, S. (2014). *Education as if Economics Mattered*. World Bank Blog http://blogs.worldbank.org/futuredevelopment/education-if-economics-mattered.

40 R. Locatelli

Moreover, education has been considered as a good which is "worthy of public debate and policy making" (Kohlrausch and Leuze 2007: 196). Indeed, as well as aspects of economic efficiency, there may be issues of equity and social justice that also justify public intervention of a redistributive nature. As argued by Amartya Sen, education, often considered as a human right and with significant public benefits, "may have a public-good component as well" (Sen 1999: 128).

As above mentioned, Ver Eecke provides a helpful contribution to addressing the uncertainty about the classification of education as a public or private good, which may also result in uncertainty concerning the role of the State in education. Education, like all other goods, may exhibit the characteristics typical of the concepts of private or public good simultaneously. Since it has undoubtedly important aspects of a public good, State intervention is required (Ver Eecke 2008; Marginson 2007).

3.2.2 What Role for the State?

Once established that education can be considered a public good, another set of issues relates to *how* the State should intervene in education. Even though a certain degree of intervention from the State is to be expected within the framework of public goods, it still remains unclear whether state functions should refer to the provision, financing and/or regulation of educational opportunities. Indeed, the economic concept of public goods does not provide a concrete guide for action (Daviet 2016).

It is acknowledged that "the government may have a role to play whenever there are important public goods. In some cases, the government may be called to provide the public goods by itself, in other cases, the government may be called to an oversight role when private groups try to realize the public good" (Ver Eecke 2008: 146). The issue of how state functions vary at different levels of education should be addressed both from an economic and political perspective. For sure, economic considerations represent an important part in the choice of solutions to the problem of public goods. As earlier mentioned, however, the discussion on public goods requires a broader reflection on socio-economic issues. Indeed, "the correct starting point of economic science must be 'political economy'" (Ver Eecke 2008: 146). A political perspective which focuses on the institutional regulation of goods may provide concrete elements which can help determine the nature and scale of state intervention when conceiving education as a public good.

These considerations partly reflect the existing human rights framework that sets out obligations for States in education and would require a more detailed analysis which, however, falls outside the scope of this work. For now, it is important to highlight that under international human rights law, education is an individual right which corresponds to positive obligations States have in order to respect, protect and fulfil this entitlement. Seeing education as a public good also implies considerations of public policy which relate to the governance of the education system. These have also to do with the way in which States relate to other actors and to how forms of privatization can or should be regulated.

3.3 The Application of the Concept of Public Goods at Different Levels of Education

The conceptualization of the principle of education as a public good however remains ambiguous. The term *education* is often used generically, without a clear distinction of how this principle should be applied according to different forms and levels. In order to understand the implications of the application of the concept of public goods at different levels of education, it is necessary to clarify what is meant by the term education and how it is being used in this work. It is clear that if understood in its broad and etymological sense, "education" means a process of "leading out" or "raising" (from the Latin: *e-ducĕre*). This understanding of education as a relational process, one that may enhance the development of free and fulfilled human beings, could hardly fall under the characteristics of the economic classification of goods, either public, merit or private. The notion of *education as a public good* mostly refers to forms of education that are somehow institutionalized either in formal or in non-formal contexts. In this sense, this concept has different implications with regard to the role of the State at different levels of education.

It can be argued that most of the references in development and human rights discourse seem to interpret education as *schooling* that should be free and compulsory. Having said this, there are also numerous applications of this concept at the level of higher education. Over the last 20 years, the academic debate on the relevance of this notion reflects the different interpretations and uses of this concept. While this book mainly focuses on basic levels of education, some reflections are also outlined regarding post-basic levels.

3.3.1 The Concept of Education As a Public Good As Outlined in Research

There have always been different interpretations of the notion of education as a public good in educational and development research. First and foremost, some authors have associated the principle of education as a public good to that of "public education" mainly in relation to basic levels. Again, there are different interpretations of what constitutes "public education". Some have argued that public education can be realized thanks to the efforts of both public and state-subsidized "private schools" (Reid 2012). Others have made a claim for public education to be a public good, understanding in this case "public education" clearly as an issue of ownership, as "publicly provided education". This interpretation is based on the assumption that market and economic approaches to education involve a weakening of democratic participation and social cohesion (Tomlinson 1986; Labaree 2000). The notion of education as a public good is understood both in the sense that education serves the public interest—"all of the members of a community have a stake in the adequate education of other people's children in that community in addition to their own" (Labaree 2000: 121)—and in the terms of education that is publicly provided.

Considering education as a public good is therefore associated to the need for public investment and public provision in the public schooling system in order to preserve equity and social justice (Riddle 2014). It is argued that the substantial public benefits of education are "supported by volumes of research, not least into the history of public education systems" (Green 2014: 28). While acknowledging the dual nature of education, represented as a private and public good at the same time—a fact that should be faced by policy-makers—it is assumed that the case should be made for education to be a public good in the interests of the majority. Indeed, according to Lewin (2015), education is a public good in the sense that its benefits extend to all. As a public good, it should be "available free at the point of service delivery" (Lewin 2015: 95). Maintaining education as a public service, while not resisting all types of reform, is considered as the best option to reduce inequalities (Green 2014). The argument is based on the idea that the State should be the ultimate guarantor of principles of social justice and equality and is therefore expected to directly commit to the provision of educational opportunities. As stated by Alexandra Draxler, "if education is a public good, then it should be non-excludable. (...) The only sector that can and might make that happen is the public sector" (Draxler 2014: 51).

It could therefore be argued that at the compulsory level, the common assumption that education is a public good has been associated to the main role of the State in the direct delivery and funding of educational opportunities (Draxler 2014; Riddle 2014). The State has always played a significant role in the development of public education systems in many parts of the world and has been directly involved in the funding and provision of education since the late eighteenth and early nineteenth centuries (Green 2014). Since the second half of the twentieth century, the expansion of the welfare state in modern societies corresponded to the expansion of education systems of which the State has been the main—and sometimes only—provider. Indeed, delivery and funding of educational opportunities have been seen as "one of the main rationales for the existence of the state" (Desai 2003: 63). Moreover, maintaining education as a public service has been considered fundamental to ensuring equity and social justice (Lewin 2015; Draxler 2014; Green 2014). This is in line with the principles underpinning the right to education, whereby States have the responsibility to ensure that at least primary education is available free to all. The right to education was included in many constitutions in both developed and developing countries, also as a result of the commitments envisaged in the Universal Declaration of Human Rights

44   R. Locatelli

(Art. 26)[3] and of the International Covenant on Economic, Social and Cultural Rights (Art. 13)[4], ratified by many countries worldwide.

However, other interpretations of the notion of education as a public good do not relate to educational provision or direct investment by the State. In the background paper prepared by the Aga Khan Foundation team for the Education for All Global Monitoring Report 2008, it is stated that "Education is a 'public good' with benefits not only to individuals, but also to society at large" (Aga Khan Foundation 2007: 7). The document provides an interesting analysis of the role of the State in education in the light of the increasing involvement of non-state actors. In the discussion on the principle of the "public good", the authors underline that "The key point [...] may be government commitment to education, rather than government necessarily doing it all" (p. 8).

The terms of the discussion change significantly when considering post-compulsory levels of education. While the right to education translates into national legislation in terms of a compulsory duration of education for all children and young people, at post-compulsory levels, it implies equality of educational opportunity and non-discrimination in access and outcomes. The question of what share of young people and adults should access different levels and types of educational provision beyond compulsory levels is a strategic policy option. For instance,

---

[3] (Article 26 UNDHR) 1. Everyone has the right to education. Education shall be free, at least in the elementary and fundamental stages. Elementary education shall be compulsory. Technical and professional education shall be made generally available, and higher education shall be equally accessible to all on the basis of merit.

2. Education shall be directed to the full development of the human personality and to the strengthening of respect for human rights and fundamental freedoms. It shall promote understanding, tolerance and friendship among all nations, racial or religious groups, and shall further the activities of the United Nations for the maintenance of peace.

3. Parents have a prior right to choose the kind of education that shall be given to their children.

[4] (Article 13 ICESCR) 1. The States Parties to the present Covenant recognize the right of everyone to education. They agree that education shall be directed to the full development of the human personality and the sense of its dignity and shall strengthen the respect for human rights and fundamental freedoms. They further agree that education shall enable all persons to participate effectively in a free society, promote understanding, tolerance and friendship among all nations and all racial, ethnic or religious groups, and further the activities of the United Nations for the maintenance of peace. 2. The States Parties to the present Covenant recognize that with a view to achieving the full realization of this right: (a) Primary education shall be compulsory and available free to all; [...]

discussion of the concept of public goods as applied to the level of higher education has mainly centred on issues of funding and on the function of higher education institutions, rather than on questions of delivery and ownership (Marginson 2011; Tilak 2009; UNESCO 2009; Calhoun 2006). Forms of state funding and regulation are considered as necessary to ensure equitable and affordable higher education.

3.3.2 Identifying the Different Roles of the State

To summarize, it could be argued that education is referred to as a public good given the need to preserve the public interest and to protect fundamental principles of equity, social cohesion and social justice. The following dimensions are outlined with regard to the functions and role of the State:

* Provision and ownership: education as a public good is often associated, although with some differences, to the notion of "public education" or "public service". It implies that the State is primarily responsible for directly providing education opportunities.
* Funding: this dimension requires the direct commitment and involvement of the State with regard to issues of financing, and it is used at both basic and post-basic levels.
* Regulation: in order to preserve the public interest, the notion of education as a public good implies that the State is the ultimate guarantor of the institutional framework, including quality assurance and setting of minimum standards to ensure equality of opportunities for all.

Having said this, the general agreement that public authorities have a duty to provide education for all, at least at basic levels, seems to be called into question by the changing educational landscape which sees the increasing involvement of non-state actors at all levels of the education process. As a result, the relevance and validity of this notion as a guiding principle for educational governance—in a context characterized by the blurring of boundaries between the public and the private, and by growing trends of for-profit education—needs to be re-contextualized.

3.4 The Blurring of Boundaries Between the Public and the Private in Education

The conceptualization of education as a public good has been called into question over the past three decades by the multiplication of public and private actors involved in education (e.g. international and national public organizations, multinational companies, non-governmental organizations [NGOs]) as well as by the diversification of sources of financing. Moreover, both the increase in the outsourcing of services and in the intervention of public institutions acting as enterprises in the market are factors which contribute to the blurring of the boundaries between what is public and what is private in education. This is characterized by different forms of interaction between the private and the public, which differ in terms of nature and significance. Examples include the opening of education institutions to for-profit purposes; the establishment of non-public institutions where investment is assured by private as well as public sponsors; the intermediation of public aid by NGOs; and so on (see Vinokur 2004). Some have argued that private sector participation in education has been encouraged indirectly by the Education 2030 agenda. According to Antonia Wulff, Coordinator at Education International, the Sustainable Development Goal (SDG) framework may favour a shift in the approach to financing, since "countries in sorting out their own financing are expected to open the door to new forms of private-sector engagement" (Wulff 2017: 57).

It is also important to note that even when education is public, compulsory and ideally free, the indirect costs borne by the households for uniforms, transportation, lunches, textbooks or for the maintenance of school buildings make the boundary between private and public education increasingly unclear. In this perspective, the categories of public and private do not appear sufficiently effective to deal with the growing diversification occurring in the global educational landscape.

The acknowledgement of a greater concern for the public sphere among the main actors involved in policy issues—the State, business, civil society organizations and households—has led to an "expansion of the public domain" (Drache 2001). In this perspective, the "public domain"—not to be confused with the public sector or with the provision of public goods—appears to be regulated by private as well as public actors, and private initiatives are somehow expected to contribute to the provision of public goods (Fig. 3.1).

These contrasts between the public and the private can lead to some apparent conflicts in defining what lies on each side of the boundary (Starr 1988). The interpenetration of sources of financing as well as of public and private decision-making raises the issue of controlling the use of public funds and especially of managing the educational system. As will be discussed in the following chapter, it is widely argued that the State cannot be counted on to optimally provide education opportunities, and private involvement is considered necessary to deal with state failure and complement state opportunities. Therefore, the notion of "public goods" becomes increasingly more difficult to define, since the State is no longer identified with the "public" but is viewed as merely another economic actor among many (Rizvi 2016).

However, its role remains relevant in the current context characterized by growing trends of privatization and commercialization of goods. Reframing the validity of the principle of education as a public good is all the more important as some forms of privatization "recast education not as a public or societal good grounded in democratic principles of justice and equal opportunity, but as an individual, atomised and personalised private good that benefits the individual and/or household" (Macpherson et al. 2014: 295).

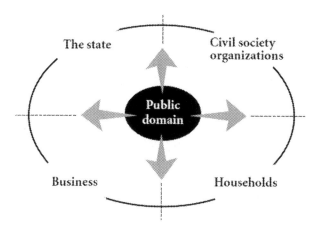

Fig. 3.1 The expanding public domain. (Source: Drache 2001)

The next chapter examines trends in education privatization which is one of the main dynamics that is characterizing the global educational landscape and contributing to the blurring of boundaries between the public and the private.

References

Adams, R. D., & McCormick, K. (1993). The Traditional Distinction Between Public and Private Goods Needs to Be Expanded, Not Abandoned. *Journal of Theoretical Politics, 5*(1), 109–116.

Aga Khan Foundation team. (2007). *Non-State Providers and Public-Private-Community Partnerships in Education.* Background paper prepared for the Education for All Global Monitoring Report 2008 *Education for All by 2015: Will we make it?* Paris: UNESCO.

Andersen, E. A., & Lindsnaes, B. (2007). *Towards New Global Strategies: Public Goods and Human Rights.* Leiden: Martinus Nijhoff Publishers.

Buchanan, J. M. (1975). *The Limits of Liberty: Between Anarchy and Leviathan.* Chicago: University of Chicago Press.

Calhoun, C. (2006). The University and the Public Good. *Thesis Eleven, 84*(1), 7–43. SAGE Publications.

Cornes, R., & Sandler, T. (1986). *The Theory of Externalities, Public Goods, and Club Goods.* New York: Cambridge University Press.

Cornes, R., & Sandler, T. (1994). Are Public Goods Myths? *Journal of Theoretical Politics, 6*(3), 369–385.

Daviet, B. (2016). *Revisiting the Principle of Education as a Public Good.* ERF Working Papers, No. 17. Paris, UNESCO Education Research and Foresight.

Desai, M. (2003). Public Goods: A Historical Perspective. In I. Kaul, P. Conceicao, K. Le Goulven, & R. U. Mendoza (Eds.), *Providing Global Public Goods: Managing Globalization* (pp. 63–77). New York: United Nations Development Programme.

Drache, D. (2001). *The Market or the Public Domain? Global Governance and the Asymmetry of Power.* London: Routledge.

Draxler, A. (2014). International Investment in Education for Development: Public Good or Economic Tool? In *Education, Learning, Training: Critical Issues for Development* (International Development Policy Series No. 5, Geneva: Graduate Institute Publications) (pp. 37–56). Boston: Brill-Nijhoff.

3 Education: A Private or Public Good?   49

Green, A. (2014). Education and the State: Whatever Happened to Education as a Public Good? *Uddannelseshistorie, 48*, 11–30.

Kaul, I., & Mendoza, R. U. (2003). Advancing the Concept of Public Goods. In I. Kaul, P. Conceicao, K. Le Goulven, & R. U. Mendoza (Eds.), *Providing Global Public Goods: Managing Globalization* (pp. 78–111). New York: United Nations Development Programme.

Kaul, I., Grunberg, I., & Stern, M. A. (1999). *Global Public Goods: International Cooperation in the 21st Century*. New York: United Nations Development Programme.

Kohlrausch, B., & Leuze, K. (2007). Implications of Marketization for the Perception of Education as Public or Private Good. In K. Martens, A. Rusconi, & K. Lutz (Eds.), *New Arenas of Education Governance* (pp. 195–213). New York: Palgrave Macmillan.

Labaree, D. F. (2000). No Exit: Public Education as an Inescapably Public Good. In L. Cuban & D. Shipps (Eds.), *Reconstructing the Common Good in Education* (pp. 110–129). Stanford, CA: Stanford University Press.

Lewin, K. M. (2015). *Educational Access, Equity, and Development: Planning to Make Rights Realities* (Fundamentals of Education Planning) (Vol. 98). Paris: UNESCO-IIEP.

Macpherson, I., Robertson, S. L., & Walford, G. (Eds.). (2014). *Education, Privatization and Social Justice: Case Studies from Africa, South Asia and South East Asia*. Oxford: Symposium Books.

Malkin, J., & Wildavsky, A. (1991). Why the Traditional Distinction Between Public and Private Goods Should Be Abandoned. *Journal of Theoretical Politics, 3*(4), 355–378.

Marginson, S. (2007). The Public/Private Divide in Higher Education: A Global Revision. *Higher Education, 53*(3), 307–333.

Marginson, S. (2011). Higher Education and Public Good. *Higher Education Quarterly, 65*(4), 411–433.

Menashy, F. (2009). Education as a Global Public Good: the Applicability and Implications of a Framework. *Globalisation, Societies and Education, 7*(3), 307–320.

Musgrave, R. (1939). Voluntary Exchange Theory of Public Economy. *The Quarterly Journal of Economics, 53*(2), 213–237.

Musgrave, R. A. (1959). *The Theory of Public Finance: A Study in Public Economy*. New York: McGraw-Hill Book Company.

Olson, M. (1965). *The Logic of Collective Action*. Cambridge, MA: Harvard University Press.

50 R. Locatelli

Razzolini, L. (2004). Public Goods. In C. K. Rowley & F. Schneider (Eds.), *The Encyclopedia of Public Choice* (Vol. 1, pp. 457–459). New York: Springer Science & Business Media.

Reid, A. (2012). Federalism, Public Education and the Public Good. In *Perspectives*. Sydney: The Whitlam Institute.

Riddle, S. (2014). *Education Is a Public Good, Not a Private Commodity*. The Conversation. Retrieved September 29, 2018, from http://theconversation.com/education-is-a-public-good-not-a-private-commodity-31408.

Rizvi, F. (2016). *Privatization in Education: Trends and Consequences*. ERF Working Papers Series, No. 18. Paris: UNESCO.

Samuelson, P. A. (1954). The Pure Theory of Public Expenditure. *The Review of Economics and Statistics, 36*(4), 387–389.

Samuelson, P. A. (1958). Aspects of Public Expenditure Theories. *Review of Economics and Statistics, 40*(4), 332–338.

Sen, A. (1999). *Development as Freedom*. New York: Anchor Books.

Smith, A. (1776). *An Inquiry into the Nature and Causes of the Wealth of Nations*. London: George Routledge and Sons.

Starr, P. (1988). The Meaning of Privatization. *Yale Law and Policy Review, 6*, 6–41.

Tilak, J. B. G. (2009). Higher Education: A Public Good or a Commodity for Trade? Commitment to Higher Education or Commitment of Higher Education to Trade. *Prospects, 38*, 449–466. Geneva, IBE- UNESCO.

Tomlinson, J. (1986). Public Education, *Public Good*. *Oxford Review of Education, 12*(3), 211–222.

UNESCO. (2009). *Communiqué - 2009 World Conference on Higher Education: The New Dynamics of Higher Education and Research For Societal Change and Development*. Paris, UNESCO.

Ver Eecke, W. (2008). *Ethical Dimensions of the Economy: Making Use of Hegel and the Concepts of Public and Merit Goods*. Berlin: Springer.

Vinokur, A. (2004). Public, privé, … ou hybride ? *Cahiers de la recherche sur l'éducation et les savoirs, 3*, 13–33.

Wulff, A. (2017). Cashing in on SDG 4. In *Spotlight on Sustainable Development 2017*. Reclaiming Policies for the Public: Privatization, Partnerships, Corporate Capture, and Their Impact on Sustainability and Inequality—Assessments and Alternatives. Report by the Civil Society Reflection Group on the 2030 Agenda for Sustainable Development (pp. 57–63). Retrieved from https://www.2030spotlight.org/sites/default/files/download/Spotlight 2017_2_4_Wulff.pdf.

4

A Changing Global Education Landscape: Growing Involvement of Non-State Actors

This chapter examines the multifaceted phenomenon of privatization and identifies tensions related to the difficulty in finding a shared definition of privatization. It provides a detailed and systematic description of how the involvement of non-state actors in education has been evolving since the beginning of the twenty-first century in different regions worldwide, especially at the compulsory level. It investigates one form of education privatization which is influenced by neo-liberal ideologies and market economics, providing an overview of the so-called Global Education Industry and its implications with regard to the governance and purposes of education.

4.1 Privatization in the Field of Education: A Complex Phenomenon

Over the last three decades, the phenomenon of privatization in the field of education has gained increasing attention in education development discourse and research. The private sector has always been involved in education, with families, religious institutions and philanthropic

© The Author(s) 2019
R. Locatelli, *Reframing Education as a Public and Common Good*,
https://doi.org/10.1007/978-3-030-24801-7_4

51

organizations playing an important role in its funding and provision. Indeed, publicly provided and funded education systems are relatively recent historical phenomena which have spread consistently in particular since the Second World War. With the emergence of the welfare state, the idea that the State has the primary responsibility for providing education "became a moral and political imperative" (Rizvi 2016: 2). In the last few decades, however, despite growing levels of public funding, "education has been increasingly funded by the private sector, often by citizens themselves" (Rizvi 2016: 3). The focus on the role of private actors has further intensified within the context of the move towards achieving Education for All (EFA). States have used privatization both to address the challenges resulting from the expansion of education at all levels and as a way to respond to the failure of governments to provide quality education. Moreover, privatization has been associated with a neo-liberal ideology which assumes that the private sector is able to provide better quality education and, when functioning as corporate or business organizations, is also more efficient in the management of the education system.

The difficulty in finding a shared understanding on this issue has different implications with regard to the assessment of the real scale of the phenomenon, as well as to the possibility of undertaking a productive discussion on the advantages or disadvantages of the increasing involvement of non-state actors in education policy and practices. Privatization has been interpreted and translated into educational practices in many ways and the forms that it takes at different levels of education vary across time and across systems, as do the rationales used to justify them.

4.1.1 The Challenges of a Shared Definition

Privatization in general is a multifaceted phenomenon which has gained wide circulation since the late 1970s and early 1980s. Privatization has been considered as a "fuzzy concept that evokes sharp political reactions [and which] covers a great range of ideas and policies, varying from the eminently reasonable to the wildly impractical" (Starr 1988: 6). One of the early definitions sees privatization as any shift from public to private in the *production* of goods and services (Starr 1988). It may include

4 A Changing Global Education Landscape: Growing... 53

policies along a spectrum of alternatives which runs from total privatization (as in government disengagement from some policy domain) to partial privatization (as in contracting out or vouchers).

In the field of education, privatization covers a wide process which encompasses a variety of forms, means, programmes and policies for its implementation (Belfield and Levin 2002; Coomans and Hallo de Wolf 2005). As for all other sectors, education privatization is a highly political issue that has been defined and interpreted in many different ways (Mazawi 2013). One of the most common definitions considers privatization as "the transfer of activities, assets and responsibilities from government/public institutions and organizations to private individuals and agencies" (Belfield and Levin 2002: 19). It is important not to confuse the process of privatization with the provision of private schooling or the generic involvement of private actors in education. Indeed, international human rights law guarantees the possibility to establish private educational institutions, as a means to ensure the freedom of parents to choose the education for their children according to their beliefs.[1] Privatization, on the other hand, implies that the State progressively diminishes its role and responsibilities with the aim of introducing higher levels of private sector participation in all domains of education, from policy-making to delivery and funding, whereas the mere establishment of a private school does not necessarily mean that there is an ongoing process of privatization.

Education privatization may occur in different forms. It may refer, either separately or simultaneously, to: (a) the increase in the number and proportion of private providers; (b) the raise in the amount of funding contributed by parents or households; (c) the enhancement of private regulation, decision-making and accountability (Belfield and Levin 2002). Privatization also refers to the outsourcing of specific state activities to private providers and to the introduction of market-based or other self-regulatory governance instruments sometimes involving forms of deregulation of the education sector (Pedró et al. 2015). Ball and Youdell distinguish between two main types of privatization trends and related policies: (a) privatization *of* public education, or "exogenous" privatization; and (b) privatization *in* public education, or "endogenous"

---

[1] Article 13(4) of the International Covenant on Economic, Social and Cultural Rights, 1966.

54 R. Locatelli

privatization. The former involves "the opening up of public education services to private sector participation on a for-profit basis and using the private sector to design, manage or deliver aspects of public education" while the latter involves the "importing of ideas, techniques and practices from the private sector in order to make the public sector more like businesses and more business-like" (Ball and Youdell 2008: 9–10). In the case of "endogenous" privatization, factors related to the influence of neoliberal ideology and of market mechanisms are taken into particular consideration.

As already stated, privatization is such a multifaceted phenomenon that some authors use the plural term *privatizations* to capture the "wide variety of types and forms of privatisation involving different financial arrangements and different relationships between funders, service providers and clients" (Ball 2007: 13). This process involves a wide variety of private stakeholders which range from parents and community-based groups to religious institutions, non-governmental organizations (NGOs) and philanthropic foundations, businesses conducting non-profit, for-profit and/or low-fee schools such as enterprises, corporations, non-philanthropic foundations and private owners (Moumné and Saudemont 2015). The private sector therefore appears as an extremely varied and evolving sector where generic considerations cannot be made and where processes and dynamics need to be examined according to different contexts.

4.1.2 Diverse Forms of Privatization

Exploration of constituent elements and distinctive features of privatization may provide a useful framework to identify the nature and scale of welfare restructuring with particular regard to education. Indeed, in welfare states, different combinations of private–public provision, as well as of funding, have given rise to various forms of privatization which contribute to a greater heterogeneity in the schooling sector. The education privatization agenda covers policies such as voucher schemes, charter schools, education sector liberalization, tax incentives, contracting out educational services, public–private partnerships and so on. It is important

4 A Changing Global Education Landscape: Growing... 55

Table 4.1 Provision versus funding in educational services

		Funding	
		Public	Private
Provision	Public	I. Traditional public schools	II. Private philanthropic ventures Tuition fees and other user fees in public schools (student loans) Private sponsorship of public schools (adopt-a-school programmes)
	Private	III. Contract schools Charter schools Voucher programmes Private school subsidy programmes Private management of public schools	IV. Fee-paying private schools Home schooling Private tutoring

Adapted from: Lewis and Patrinos (2012), LaRocque (2008) and Verger (2012)

to note that as education is increasingly regarded as an industry, its key features have acquired the form of other market-driven enterprises with terms such as "contract", "voucher" and "liberalization" now included in the vocabulary of education (Rizvi 2016). Table 4.1 exemplifies different options that result from the combinations of public–private/funding–provision in the field of education, through which public authorities can engage with the private sector.

This table exemplifies the complexity of education privatization whereby mixed models exist along with fully public education and fully private education.

4.1.3 The Political and Social Dimensions of Privatization

While prevailing definitions of privatization have been considered mainly in their administrative, economic and technical dimensions, it is also important to consider the social and political dimensions of privatization, because they can have a profound impact on education opportunities.

56   R. Locatelli

Indeed, privatization processes not only change the way schools are managed, financed, but also how they are governed, and held accountable (Scott and DiMartino 2009: 433). Thus, a discussion on the shift towards privatization in education should include issues such as the participation and influence of private actors in the education decision-making process. Moreover, socio-cultural implications should also be debated as privatization may change the underlying political values, understandings and capacity for action in society (Wells and Scott 2001). This is particularly relevant as some forms of privatization give more prominence to the individual economic benefits of education rather than to collective social and civic aims, with implications regarding the values and purposes of education as a private or a public good.

In order to analyse the complexity of privatization in current welfare systems, it is important to consider, beyond dimensions of funding and provision, issues relating to the decision-making process, which can be either public or private. Based on a classification that Burchardt refers to as "wheel of welfare" (1997), it is possible to see different combinations of public and private provision, public and private finance and public and private decision-making (see Fig. 4.1). Indeed, while the table illustrated earlier (see Table 4.1) classifies combinations of public and private on the basis of the two dimensions of provision and funding, the three-dimensional figure takes also into account the decision-making process, which can be either public or private.[2]

This chart provides a more comprehensive representation of the phenomenon of privatization as it includes, in each of the four sectors identified in Table 4.1, a further subdivision relating to the decision-making process. Indeed, some forms of privatization lead to a shift in accountability from public to private actors. Another aspect that should be considered relates to the way education systems are *regulated*. This is particularly relevant in the context of increasing involvement of private sector providers in publicly funded services, since one of the ways in which policy-makers may seek to safeguard the public purse is to impose tight

---

[2] The original, and more detailed chart, can be found in: Burchardt (1997). Boundaries between public and private welfare: a typology and map of services. *CASE Paper/2*, Centre for Analysis of Social Exclusion, London School of Economics.

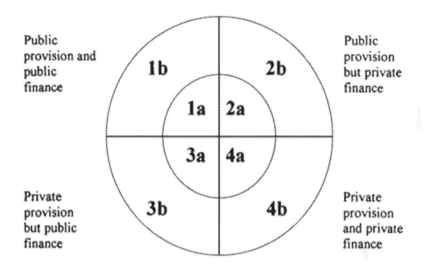

Key

Inner Circle – public decision

1a   eg 'pure public' services
2a   eg publicly provided services paid for by user charges
3a   eg contracted-out services purchased by the State
4a   eg contracted-out services paid for by consumer

Outer Circle – private decision

1b   eg publicly provided services bought with vouchers
2b   eg publicly provided services bought by individuals
3b   eg privately provided services bought with vouchers, tax reliefs or grants
4b   eg 'free market' services

Fig. 4.1 Classification of public and private welfare activity. (Source: Burchardt et al. 1999)

58   R. Locatelli

Table 4.2 The multifaceted phenomenon of privatization

Administrative
Shift in the management of economic and human resources
Technical
Greater reliance on private regulation and monitoring
Economic
Shift from public to private provision and/or financing of educational services
Political
Increasing participation/influence of private actors in the education decision-making process. Greater responsibilities for non-state actors, potential changes in the governance of education
Social/cultural
Changes in the underlying political values, understandings, and capacities for action in society.

regulations on providers. Since all regulation is public, the range of the regulation dimension would presumably be "more–less" rather than "public–private". It may be useful to focus on the degree of regulation to which the privately provided, privately decided subsector is subject and how this has changed over time, as some forms of privatization develop without control of the State, leading to privatization of the governance itself.

Table 4.2 illustrates the administrative, technical, economic, social and political dimensions of the multifaceted phenomenon of privatization.

As discussed earlier, traditional definitions of privatization mainly relate to the red parts of the table, considering administrative, technical or economic facets. However, it is evident that privatization is not only about shifts in the modes of ownership and funding of educational provision but also about who controls and manages the distribution of educational resources (Mazawi 2013). Therefore, privatization is inevitably linked to the blue fields as well, since it has a direct influence on both the political and the socio-cultural domains. As such, privatization is so involved in wider social and political struggles among a range of social and corporate actors that the "traditional, formalist" distinction between public and private sectors in relation to privatization has somehow collapsed (Mazawi 2013).

4.2 What Is "Public" and "Private" in Education?

It has been argued that the habitual principal difference between the definition of the public and the private in education is becoming less evident due to the ever-increasing interconnection between different forms and practices in privatization policies, the multiplication of public and private actors involved in education (e.g. international and national public organizations, multinational companies, NGOs) as well as the diversification of sources of financing (UNESCO 2015a; Kitaev 1999; Ball 2007; Olmedo 2016). Indeed, it has been suggested that "the definition of 'private' is by no means clear-cut in situations where many 'private' schools are heavily funded and regulated by the state", representing a "continuum of public and private funding and control" (Kitaev 1999: 41). Identifying what is public and private can therefore be a source of frustration since, behind legal categories of public and private, the boundaries are blurred (Starr 1988).

A further source of frustration with the public/private distinction is that the terms do not have consistent meanings from one institutional sphere to another. In the United States, for instance, the difference between public and private schools is not the same as the difference between public and private broadcasting. An American public school is public, not only in that it is owned and financed by the State but also because it is open to all children of eligible age in a given area. Public is to private not only as state is to non-state but also as open is to closed (Starr 1988). Along the same lines, public education is sometimes referred to by some as all education that is provided and funded by public authorities, whereas for others public education can be realized thanks to the efforts of both public and state-subsidized "private schools" (Reid 2012). Private education has been generally defined as

all formal schools that are *not* public, and may be founded, owned, managed and financed by actors other than the state, even in cases when the state provides most of the funding and has considerable control over these schools (teachers, curriculum, accreditations, etc.) (Kitaev 1999: 43)

60   R. Locatelli

This definition highlights the complexity of distinguishing between private/public institutions in education, where different arrangements are possible in relation to provision/financing/regulation as above mentioned. These contrasts between the public and the private lead to some apparent conflicts in defining what lies on each side of the boundary, contributing to the creation of some forms that are hybrid (Starr 1988). In this respect, it should be specified that this blurred vision may result in a lack of clarity in terms of roles and responsibilities among the different actors involved in education, with important consequences for the role of the State as the primary guarantor of education as a public good.

Focusing on the classification of educational institutions, it has been argued that according to legal criteria, categories of "public" and "private" refer either to issues of ownership and financing or to issues of management and regulation thereof (Vinokur 2004). With regard to issues of ownership and financing, a *public* institution is one that provides free education services and is owned and funded by the State or a public authority. A *private* institution can be either for profit or not and can therefore provide either free or marketable education. Private educational institutions are owned by non-state, private actors and are generically submitted to the monitoring of public authorities (Vinokur 2004).

Categories of public and private can also be identified by taking into account criteria of management and regulation of educational institutions. The UNESCO (United Nations Educational, Scientific and Cultural Organization) International Institute for Educational Planning identifies criteria of control and management as determinants for establishing public or private institutions (Kitaev 2001). This clearly recalls the definition provided by the UNESCO Institute for Statistics which classifies educational institutions as public or private "depending on the body which has *overall control* of the institution and not according to which sector provides the majority of the funding" (UIS 2016: 18). It follows that:

"A **public** institution is one that is controlled and managed directly by a public education authority or agency of the country where it is located or by a government agency directly or by a governing body (council, committee, etc.), most of whose members are either appointed by a public authority of the country where it is located or elected by public franchise."

4 A Changing Global Education Landscape: Growing... 61

"A **private** institution is one that is controlled and managed by a non-governmental organization (e.g. a church, a trade union or a business enterprise, foreign or international agency), or its governing board consists mostly of members who have not been selected by a public agency."

The definition of the Organisation for Economic Co-operation and Development (OECD) is aligned to that of the UNESCO Institute for Statistics. According to the OECD, the classification of public and private is made according to whether a public agency or a private entity has the *ultimate* control over the institution (OECD 2004).

In these cases, the demarcation line consists in the control and managing function of these institutions, whereas property or financing criteria are not taken directly into account. Therefore, the participation of the families in the financing of education may be interpreted as a form of privatization when the criteria adopted refer to property and financing. Considering the criteria of management and regulation, the participation of families may represent a form of privatization when the school is controlled and managed by the parents themselves or if the directors have not been elected by public vote (Vinokur 2004). Moreover, the public financing provided to education institutions is key in determining an institution as "public" only when the criteria considered are those of property and financing, whereas according to the definitions of the UNESCO Institute for Statistics or of the OECD, a public institution is as such irrespectively of private or public funding.

It is evident that a common definition of public and private institution or school remains unclear (UNESCO 2016: 188). The adoption of different criteria for the classification of private and public in education has implications on the real representation of private involvement and its consequences for the governance of education. When considering the criteria of ownership and funding, figures may provide significant information about the distribution and flow of funds as well as the scale of privately owned institutions. However, the adoption of these criteria may not appear sufficiently satisfactory with regard to issues of governance, notably of control and regulation that may affect the way schools are operated by private or public institutions. At the same time, criteria of management and control, as adopted by UNESCO and the OECD, may provide a more significant analysis for the assessment of private and public institutions regarding who is ultimately responsible for regulation and governance, but may lack important elements that the other two criteria do provide. Moreover, it is also crucial to underline that definitions of private institutions do not distinguish between for-profit and not-for-profit schools nor identify if they are fee-paying or free of charge. The difficulty of identifying common tools to apply to the analysis on the issue of privatization is not irrelevant as it may incur a certain degree of difficulty in the building and assessment of the true scale of the phenomenon.

Having said this, throughout this work, concepts of public and private educational institutions are aligned to the definitions provided by the UNESCO Institute of Statistics. This is essential in order to refer to data and trends which are mostly issued by this institution. However, a clarification needs to be provided with respect to the definition of *private* institutions which should be submitted to the monitoring of public authority, and their freedom should be limited by the regulatory function of the State. Even where schools are owned and managed by the private sector, they are often subsidized by the government who pays the costs of curriculum development, inspection and examinations. In most cases, the State attempts to maintain some control over all education institutions (both private and public) through regulation. In addition, clarifications will be made when different criteria, rather than those of control and management, are used.

4.3 Trends of Privatization at Different Levels in Different Regions Worldwide

The trend towards the privatization of education is growing at all levels across the world (UNESCO 2015a). The indicator relating to the share of enrolment in private institutions provides one significant measure to estimate the complex trends of privatization. In the last three decades, the proportion of children going to private institutions at the primary level has risen worldwide from around 8 per cent to more than 17 per cent, and this trend is continuing to grow (UIS [UNESCO Institute for

4 A Changing Global Education Landscape: Growing... 63

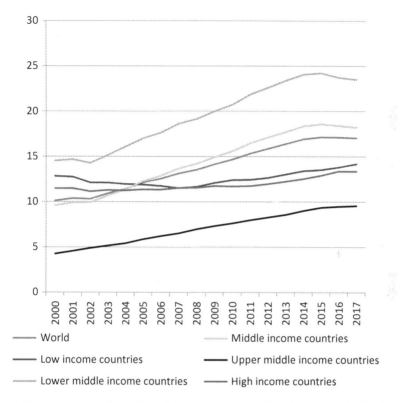

Fig. 4.2 Percentage of enrolment in primary education in private institutions (UIS database)

Statistics] database). In general, the most significant increase of enrolment in private schools has occurred since the year 2000, probably as a result of the growing attention paid to achieving universal primary education.[3]

Lower middle-income countries is where this share has increased most, and in 2017, it was approximately one-third higher than the world average (see Fig. 4.2).

---

[3] This was the focus of the education-related goal of the Millennium Development Agenda and of the Education for All movement which, although not only focusing at the primary level, ended by promoting universal primary education.

This growth is even more apparent at the secondary level where the share of private enrolments in lower middle-income countries is almost double the world average. This can be attributed to the significant demographic and social changes and to the corresponding inability of the State to face growing demands for education (UNESCO 2015a) (Fig. 4.3).

Among the lower middle-income countries, South and West Asia are the regions where this proportion has increased the most at both primary and secondary levels between 2000 and 2017, representing almost double the world average (UIS database). In South Asia, by 2017, Nepal had

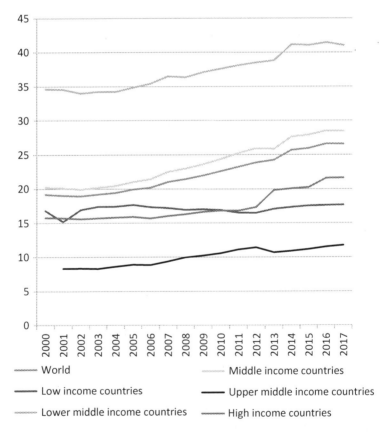

Fig. 4.3 Percentage of enrolment in secondary education in private institutions (UIS database)

4 A Changing Global Education Landscape: Growing... 65

increased this share from 6 per cent to more than 15 per cent at primary level while Bangladesh, India and Pakistan had far exceeded the regional average (Bhatta and Pherali 2017).

Although to a lesser extent, the trend has been constantly increasing also in other regions of the world. In Latin America and the Caribbean, the share has increased from around 13 per cent up to more 20 per cent at the primary level, with countries such as Peru[4] experiencing a considerable increase with this share almost doubling between 2000 and 2017. Arab States have also witnessed a significant increase in the enrolment in private schools especially at the primary level, where this share has risen from around 6 to almost 9 per cent (UIS database). It should be noted however that this region is characterized by significant economic disparities and privatization may be the effect of different drivers. Indeed, this share is particularly high in Lebanon, where there is a long history of private schooling, and in the countries of the Arabian Peninsula such as Bahrain, Qatar and in the United Arab Emirates. Although this share is not so high in Morocco as compared to these countries, it has increased by four between 2000 and 2017, rising from around 4 per cent to more than 16 per cent (UIS database).

While in Sub-Saharan Africa the share of enrolment in private primary schools did not increase significantly during the same period—rising from around 10 per cent to almost 14 per cent between 2000 and 2017 (UIS database)—it is important to note that there are countries in this region where the numbers of enrolments in primary education in private institutions are particularly impressive. Countries such as Uganda, Burkina Faso, Senegal, DR Congo, Kenya, Nigeria and Ghana have seen this share increasing twofold or even more, and the trend is continuing to grow.[5] It should also be noted that information is missing in many countries and, even when available, administrative data tend to underestimate the share of private school enrolment, especially in countries where

---

[4] In Peru, it raised from around 16 per cent to more than 29 per cent (UIS database).

[5] It has almost doubled in Uganda, from around 10 per cent to 19 per cent, in Burkina Faso from 11 per cent to 20 per cent, in Nigeria from 6 per cent to 12 per cent, in Senegal from 10 per cent to 16 per cent, Congo from 0.35 per cent to 31.07 per cent, Kenya from 4 per cent to almost 16 per cent, and in Ghana from 17 per cent to 25 per cent (data retrieved from the UIS database).

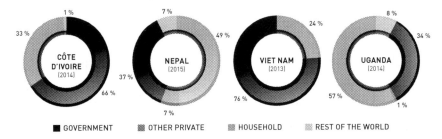

Fig. 4.4 Total funding for education by source. (Source: UIS and IIEP 2016)

the private sector is expanding and some schools operate without official recognition (Wodon 2014).[6]

The share of private enrolment in primary schools not only varies within regions but also within countries. For instance, while the share of enrolment in primary schools in Nigeria stood at about 24 per cent in 2015, in the state of Lagos, over 60 per cent of primary students were enrolled in private schools (Härmä 2011). Distribution of enrolments also varies within cities themselves. In Kisumu, the third largest city in Kenya, most of primary schools are located in the city centre, since richer people live there. Public schools represent 70 per cent of total primary institutions. However, while public schools are distributed in the territory of the city, 30 per cent of private schools are mostly concentrated in the central part of the city (Viteri 2016).

It is important to remember that, when adopting the criterion of *funding*, privatization may also occur when there is a shift from public to private financing. An interesting analysis of the contribution of families to education spending conducted by the UNESCO Institute for Statistics (UIS) provides a clearer understanding of which public and private actors invest more in education. The National Education Accounts (NEA) methodology was developed by the UIS in order to provide a more complete picture of education financing flows, with regard to different levels of education and all sources of funding, including households'. According

---

[6] For instance, in Nigeria, private schools accounted for 5 per cent of primary enrolment in 2005 and 8 per cent in 2010, according to the UNESCO Institute for Statistics. Yet survey data indicate the share was already 13 per cent in 2004 and reached 24 per cent by 2015 (NPC and Macro 2004; Nigeria NPC and RTI International 2016).

to the NEA analysis, governments are not always the most important funders of education. In two of the countries analysed, Nepal and Uganda, "households are major but often forgotten contributors to education funding" (UIS and IIEP 2016) (see Fig. 4.4).

It should be underlined that a high proportion of household spending is concentrated at non-primary levels. Primary education receives the largest share of expenditure from government sources in almost all countries in the survey, while other levels receive more private funding. The NEA analysis also provides a more detailed exploration of household expenditure. Fees and payments to schools are the most significant items in private schools. However payments made outside of schools for items such as uniforms, teaching materials, private classes and other expenses (also referred to as "indirect cost") often represent more than one-half of what households spend on education, also in public schools (UIS and IIEP 2016). Considering the high burden of education on family budgets, the UNESCO Institute of Statistics has recently published a guidebook for designing household survey questionnaires in order to estimate more accurately household expenditure on education.[7]

This section has aimed at drawing a more subtle picture of the complex phenomenon of education privatization. Indeed, official data collected at national level may hide significant disparities in the distribution of private schools within countries, regions and cities themselves. When looking at the phenomenon of privatization, all features should be observed, including the contribution of households to education expenditure. This has an enormous impact on the level of fairness and equity in the education system.

4.4 Rationales for Education Privatization

There are several driving forces behind the process of privatization in the field of education. Factors and rationales differ in intensity and in nature between countries leading to different types of privatization. It has been

---

[7] *Measuring Household Expenditure on Education: A Guidebook for designing household survey questionnaires* (2018). http://uis.unesco.org/sites/default/files/documents/measuring-household-expenditure-education-2018-en.pdf.

68   R. Locatelli

argued that in developed countries, the provision of private schools is nearly always the result of a quest for a diversified demand for education and of the deliberate choice of an alternative to the public system, whereas in developing countries, the development of private solutions is often stimulated by unmet demand and an inadequate public offering (Kitaev 2001). However, rationales and factors are not so clear-cut between developing and developed countries. For instance, parental choice is often mentioned as one of the main justifications for the growing offer of privatization in developed and developing countries alike (Belfield and Levin 2002).

For the purposes of this analysis, the different motivations behind privatization can be explained according to the following issues:

* Growing demand for more diversified educational opportunities
* Government failure to provide quality education for all its citizens
* Globalization and the spread of neoliberal ideology

The following sections analyse in detail each of these "driving forces" in order to draw a comprehensive picture of the rationales driving the phenomenon of education privatization.

4.4.1 Growing Demand for More Diversified Educational Opportunities

Although the factors leading to privatization are highly interconnected, the growth of private engagement in education may be the result of both an "excess demand" and a "diversified demand" (Belfield and Levin 2002). Education is often considered by parents as a key instrument for social and economic improvement/advancement as they seek to provide the best opportunity for their children. Moreover, the growth in living standards, as well as the structure of economies and societies becoming more specialized, has fuelled a differentiated demand for schools. These factors may cater for the needs not met by public schools, increasingly perceived as providing standardized, uniform education (Belfield and Levin 2002). Indeed, the growth of enrolments in private schools has also

4 A Changing Global Education Landscape: Growing... 69

been associated to rising incomes which have followed steady economic growth in recent years, as well as to increased levels of education among parents and in some cases to apparently low or declining quality in the public sector (Rolleston and Adefeso-Olateju 2014).

Along with the Education for All and the Millennium Development Goals global agendas, the increasing demand for education has contributed to an expansion of access to education and to the lengthening of the average duration of schooling across the world. Since 2000, the length of compulsory education has expanded significantly, rising by one-fourth or even one-third in many countries worldwide (UIS database). Indeed, the first target of Sustainable Development Goal 4 stipulates the provision of 12 years of free public primary and secondary education of which at least 9 should be compulsory.

With the lengthening of compulsory education, the number of children enrolled in primary school has increased worldwide by almost 10 per cent, rising from 82 per cent in 2000 to more than 91 per cent in 2017 (UIS database). This trend is particularly significant in Sub-Saharan Africa, where this figure has risen by almost 20 points, from around 60 per cent in 2000 to almost 80 per cent in 2017. Within the same timeframe, significant changes in enrolments have also taken place in the Arab States and in South and West Asia where figures have risen from 79 to 88 per cent in the former and to 93 per cent in the latter (UIS database). At the secondary level, there has also been a significant increase in enrolment especially in some regions of the world. In South and West Asia, the number of children and adolescents enrolled in lower secondary schools increased from 61 to more than 82 per cent between 2000 and 2017. In Sub-Saharan Africa too, the enrolment level has increased substantially, but even so, at 64 per cent it still remains at the lowest worldwide.

The growth in enrolment is also the result of significant demographic changes which have occurred worldwide (UNESCO 2015a). Total population has increased by more than one billion in the last 15 years and is estimated to continue growing, although at a slower rate. By 2030, it is expected that the total population will increase by a further one billion, reaching 8.5 billion people. It is important to consider that the increase in population has been unevenly distributed, most of it taking place in low and lower middle-income countries, especially in sub-Saharan Africa and Southern Asia (UNESCO 2016).

The resulting expansion of access to education at all levels has generated greater pressures on public schooling systems in terms of both funding and delivery of education opportunities. Indeed, the expansion of demand for education has put greater pressure on government budgets in a period of economic crisis, especially in countries where financial and taxation systems are not fully set up. Private funding has been therefore increasingly considered as a necessary complement to the already constrained public budgets.

4.4.2 Government Failure to Provide Quality Basic Education for All Its Citizens

It is argued that dissatisfaction towards public education systems and a potential "government failure" that may result from financial constraints, excessive bureaucracy and inefficiency, could also help to illustrate the reasons for private education development (Kitaev 1999).

Despite the increasing enrolment in education at all levels, many children still do not have access to primary school. The UNESCO Institute of Statistics estimates that since 2008 the number of out-of-school children and adolescents has stalled at 263 million, which includes 64 million of primary school age (9 per cent), 61 million adolescents of lower secondary school age (16 per cent) and 138 million young people of upper secondary school age (36 per cent). Due in part to high growth rates in population, more than half of out-of-school children at the primary school level live in Sub-Saharan Africa (34 million), representing more than 20 per cent of the children living in the region (UIS and UNESCO 2016). Moreover, the most marginalized children—including the poorest, children with disabilities, girls and those from cultural or linguistic minorities—are being disproportionately left behind. Equity in education has still not been achieved, with girls still not enrolled in primary school at an equal rate as boys, and with the highest out-of-school rates among the poorest households (UIS and UNESCO 2016).

Moreover, even when children have access to schools, incomplete schooling and poor quality education contribute to insufficient levels of acquisition of basic skills. According to UIS data, "[i]n a quarter of the

4 A Changing Global Education Landscape: Growing... 71

world's countries, less than half of children are learning basic literacy and numeracy skills, and about 80% of those not learning these basic skills live in sub-Saharan Africa. In total, 250 million children are not learning the basics" (UNESCO 2014: 301). The number and distribution of teachers are important policy parameters that help to determine the quality of education. The pupil–trained teacher[8] ratio is an indicator that reflects the capacity of education systems in terms of trained human resources. High ratios—exceeding 40:1 in primary education and 25:1 in secondary education—signify overcrowded classrooms and an overloaded teaching workforce. Most countries with more than 40 pupils per teacher in primary education are in sub-Saharan Africa (UIS database).

In order to put greater emphasis on the learning crisis which affects many poor countries worldwide, in the years preceding the adoption of the new global agenda for education, several international organizations encouraged a shift from a focus on mere "'access" to education to a focus on access *plus* learning. It should be stressed that the promotion and value of learning has had a long tradition in international education debate since the 1970s.[9] Having said this, it is true that the subsequent focus in international educational development has been on the *access* to formal education (within the Education for All movement, and even more so

---

[8] According to the UNESCO Institute for Statistics, "a trained teacher has 'at least the minimum organized teacher training requirements (pre-service or in-service) to teach a specific level of education according to the relevant national policy or law'. The requirements usually include pedagogical knowledge (approaches, methods and techniques of teaching) and professional knowledge (instruments and legal frameworks governing the teaching profession). Some programs may also cover content knowledge (curriculum, subject matter and use of relevant materials" (UNESCO 2016: 330).

[9] The idea of lifelong learning (at that time called lifelong education), for instance, was first introduced as early as 1972 through the landmark publication, *Learning to Be: Education in the World of Today and Tomorrow*. The Education for All (EFA) movement launched in Jomtien, Thailand, in 1990 was based on a collective commitment to meet the basic *learning* needs of all. Several years later, the 1996 publication, *Learning: The Treasure Within*, commonly referred to as the *Delors Report*, proposed an integrated vision of education based on the four pillars of learning to be, to know, to do, and to live together. The Dakar Framework of Action in 2000 also contributed to the idea that *learning* constituted a cornerstone for the EFA Agenda, as it was 'designed to enable all individuals to realize their right to learn ...' (2000: 29). In particular, Goal 6 of Education for All commits world leaders to: 'Improving every aspect of the quality of education, and ensuring their excellence so that recognized and measurable learning outcomes are achieved by all ...', a clear example of how the goals set out in the Agenda were already much respondent to the notions of quality education and of learning.

within Millennium Development Goals agendas), with little attention given to the quality of *learning*. As illustrated above, despite expanding access to primary education, basic learning levels are frequently very low. In addition, the need to respond to high economic constraints has resulted in a quest for more efficient ways of governing education systems, hence the centrality and urgency of assessing the quality of education and of learning outcomes. In response, many have called on countries and the international community to work together to improve *quality* and *learning* which have become key principles of the Goal 4 of the 2030 Agenda for Sustainable Development: *Ensure inclusive and equitable quality education and promote lifelong learning opportunities for all.*

Mismanagement, lack of accountability and corruption are also symptoms of the so-called government failure, that is, imperfection in government performance (Orbach 2013). It has been argued that "government[s] should be credited for recognizing the failure to achieve learning outcomes, despite increased resources being made available" (UNESCO 2015b: 257). The lack of transparency of many public authorities has led to increasing demands for participation and accountability, particularly in light of corruption and inefficiency in education systems and failure to deliver basic services despite greater investment (UNESCO 2015b). In addition, recent estimates suggest that developing countries lose about US$100 billion annually in revenue from multinational tax avoidance through offshore investments (UNCTAD 2015). "Illicit financial flows, defined as illegal movements of money or capital between countries, are symptoms of governance failures, weak institutions and corruption" (UNESCO 2016: 135).

Against this backdrop, the private sector is often considered more efficient in the management of the education system and in the provision of higher quality education where class overcrowding, which is often a feature of public schools, is avoided. Private schools are also seen as more accountable than government ones, enhancing greater transparency of the education process. Indeed, beyond economic considerations, a range of other values also influence parents' educational choices. These include educational, social, religious and moral values. Evaluation of the relationships between teachers and parents, the responsibility and accountability of schools to parents and pupils, the use of corporal punishment, and the availability of extra-curricular and enrichment activities are all considerations that refer to the so-called calculus of care[10] which often replaces mere economic considerations in the choice of schools (Rolleston and Adefeso-Olateju 2014). According to a study of the UK Department for International Development, there is consistent evidence that in private schools, users participate in and influence decision-making more than in private schools (Ashley et al. 2014). Moreover, it is considered that better quality education is achieved also thanks to greater teacher accountability to employers in private schools than in the public sector where their teaching is considered substandard and they fail to attend school regularly (Walford 2011). Although this issue is highly debated, and "much of the evidence [...] also indicates that private school teachers are often less formally qualified, have low salaries and weak job security" (Ashley et al. 2014: 19), the resulting impression of greater accountability is a feature that the public sector should take into serious consideration.

4.4.3 The Spread of Neo-liberal Ideology

Globalization and the expansion of the neo-liberal ideology which has been spreading since the 1980s are considered the main factors shaping current forms of education privatization worldwide and influencing both supply and demand pressures across the world. Neo-liberalism has become to some degree a system of thought, a model of reason that frames human interactions mainly in economic terms (Rizvi 2016). This phenomenon has led to a greater market involvement in the education sector. Indeed, despite the fact that the use of the private sector in education has a long history, "what is new about these manifestations is their *scale, scope* and *penetration* into almost all aspects of the education endeavour" (Macpherson et al. 2014: 9)—education is increasingly conceptualized as a commodity and the learner as a consumer (Robertson and Verger 2012; Labaree 2011).

More explicitly, education is increasingly valued for its contribution to the process of capital formation, whereas the citizen is considered as a

---

[10] This expression is used by Noddings (2005) to emphasize the importance of an 'ethic of care' in an increasingly achievement-oriented educational environment.

mere investor and consumer and not as a member of a society expressing a specific set of values, experiences and traditions (Rizvi 2016). Within a neo-liberal economic perspective, the education discourse is characterized by an instrumentalist human capital theory, as formulated by T.W. Schultz and Gary Becker in the 1960s. Human capital theory provides education with an explicit economic value, seeing it as an important explanation for economic progress. In this perspective, education is considered a good investment in terms of human capital, especially with regard to the benefits, the greater earning capacity and other advantages to the individual that education would enhance (Rizvi 2016). This phenomenon appears not only to privatize the production and consumption of goods that were once publicly financed and provided but also to recast the purposes of education and its organization. For all these reasons, this particular form of privatization, also referred to as marketization, should be dealt with more closely.

In dealing with the phenomenon of the growing engagement of the private in education, it is therefore important to identify, beyond economic rationales, the highly political nature of privatization itself (Rizvi and Lingard 2010). Within the last three decades, educational privatization has been attached to an ideological assumption about the superiority of the private sector over the public, especially with regard to remedying what many conservative and neo-liberal advocates consider as the failure of public schools to provide excellent education given public resource allocations (Scott and DiMartino 2009; Rizvi and Lingard 2010). This ideology differs from the liberal economic approach as coined by Adam Smith, who conceived the State as having a major role to play in the intellectual and moral education of the people (Laval 2003). It is today a more radical version of the liberal doctrine, as theorized in the work of Milton Friedman (2002 [1962]) and, later, in that of Chubb and Moe (1990), which legitimizes business engagement in the big educational market. In contrast to Keynesian policies which encouraged a strong intervention of the State for reconstruction after Second World War , advocates of neo-liberalism consider the private sector as a necessary tool to increase competition, generate efficiency and innovation in all sectors of society (Robertson and Verger 2012; Scott and DiMartino 2009; Rizvi and Lingard 2010).

4 A Changing Global Education Landscape: Growing... 75

In general, neo-liberalism questions State intervention in the direct production of goods and services, be they transportation, health or education and deems its appropriate role limited to the regulation and preservation of an institutional framework. Milton Friedman already addressed the debate of government intervention in the field of education in a famous article in 1955.[11] While he considered governmental financing in the early years of education appropriate, due to the positive externalities of education for citizenship—or what he called the "neighbourhood effects"—he did not justify direct government involvement in the administration of schools. He considered the *voucher scheme* as the best option to respect parents' freedom of choice thanks to increased competition between different types of public and private schools. These approaches resulted in a series of national and local deregulatory policies (Scott and DiMartino 2009). In this perspective, the role of the State would be limited to ensuring the quality of the service provided by private schools. As Milton Friedman concludes:

> The result of these measures would be a sizable reduction in the direct activities of government, yet a great widening in the educational opportunities open to our children. They would bring a healthy increase in the variety of educational institutions available and in competition among them. Private initiative and enterprise would quicken the pace of progress in this area as it has in so many others. Government would serve its proper function of improving the operation of the invisible hand without substituting the dead hand of bureaucracy. (1955)

For advocates of neo-liberal ideology, a shift from public control to market control of schooling is considered desirable in order to make schools more efficient and effective. The political rationale underpinning the vision of education as a public good, one that implies a strong role of the State and sees education as necessary for achieving public and societal aims, is shifted to a market rationale, which considers education as an individual private and consumable good (Labaree 2011). This phenomenon has acquired a global scale and is affecting the ways and forms in which decisions in education are made, and how it is provided, funded and regulated.

---

[11] Milton Friedman. 1955. *The Role of Government in Education*, available at www.schoolchoices.org/roo/fried1.htm.

4.5 Marketization and the "Global Education Industry"

Since the 1980s, the aims of neo-liberal ideology have been translated into policies marking shifts towards greater reliance on the mechanisms of the market in the management of social services and goods such as education. It was suggested that, without privatization, the tax burden on citizens could not be reduced, making it difficult for them to choose whether or not to buy the services they needed or wanted. Many of these arguments were further developed in theories of "New Public Management"[12] which suggested that the business ideas that had proved successful in the private sector could also be applied to the management of public services (Rizvi 2016). These reforms were adopted in several countries "across the West" and promoted in developing countries especially in Latin America (Ball and Youdell 2008). With specific attention on outputs and performance rather than on inputs and process, these reforms fostered private engagement in the field of education and encouraged the idea that schools could be easily "managed" as private companies. The approach of "educational management" consisted in bringing a set of methods, ideals and concepts from the private to the public sector. The planning of educational objectives, the management of human resources, the adoption of accountability systems and of common core standards opened market opportunities to a broad range of edu-businesses (Ball and Youdell 2008; Verger et al. 2016).

These changes have been blending the public and private sectors to the extent of considering education a "quasi-market" (Belfield and Levin 2002; Kitaev 1999; Ball and Youdell 2008; Labaree 2011; Whitty and Power 2000). According to Belfield and Levin (2002), the "quasi-market" envisages that the government maintains an important role in terms of accountability and quality assurance. Its activity is, however, completed by private-sector mechanisms such as competition among suppliers of

---

[12] The term "New Public Management" was coined by Christopher Hood (1991) to refer to a clustering of elements that included performance targets, specification of standards and indicators, results-driven allocations, inspection and the outsourcing of a range of activities that had once been a central part of the public sector.

4 A Changing Global Education Landscape: Growing... 77

educational services; regulation of entry and exit from schooling; introduction of voucher or funding mechanisms that encourage policies of choice. The concepts of privatization and marketization are therefore highly interconnected. It is argued that, although "privatisation does not in itself constitute market relations, it creates a potentially favourable environment for market activity" (Whitty and Power 2000: 178). Yet, beyond privatization, we are witnessing today an increasing marketization of education, a "general shift to the embrace of business-oriented principles and highlights" (Cucchiara et al. 2011), a shift which has been occurring on a global scale, and has been promoted by international organizations and private actors which are progressively playing a key role in the governance of education worldwide.

4.5.1 The Global Scale of Market Engagement

Growing trends in globalization have led to a greater trans-nationalization of education policies, also referred to as "policyscapes" (Carney 2009) or policies that are no longer understood only in the context of national decision-making. "Globalization, linked with market liberalization, has both pressured and encouraged governments to seek more efficient, more flexible, and more expansive education systems" (Belfield and Levin 2002: 32). States have been increasingly involved in a global economy where rules and paradigms are highly influenced by neo-liberal ideology. Indeed, despite the different social, political, historical and economic traditions, there is remarkable similarity in the ways in which nations have addressed respective issues in the governance of education (Rizvi 2016).

This is also the result of increased attention in the field of education on the part of international organizations and aid agencies which, since the 1980s, have encouraged reforms towards privatization of the education systems by giving assistance in many developing countries (Klees et al. 2012; Belfield and Levin 2002). The comparative policy work of international organizations such as the OECD, the World Bank and UNESCO has become increasingly influential. Regional and global policy networks have risen, leading to greater levels of cooperation across nation-states whose policies are increasingly characterized by a common set of interests and policy priorities.

78   R. Locatelli

Education has been considered as a "miracle cure" (Klees 2012) by the World Bank, whose investment in primary education increased consistently and represented one-quarter of its total loans by the end of 1970s. From a historical perspective, the cluster of policies and practices implemented over the 1980s, and inspired by dominant neoliberal ideology, came to be referred to, in policy and development, circles as the Washington Consensus.[13] It consisted in a set of ten economic policy prescriptions promoted for developing countries by Washington, D.C.-based institutions such as the International Monetary Fund (IMF), the World Bank and the US Treasury Department.[14] These "Washington institutions" (Rose 2003) have dominated development practices over the last three decades adopting a restrictive economic view with regard to development. Policy instruments are reflected in the Structural Adjustment Programs (SAPs)[15] implemented by the World Bank and by the International Monetary Fund, which aimed to rely on market forces and reduce State intervention and expenditure in the field of education to a minimum (Ball and Youdell 2008; Rose 2003). These Programmes have been highly criticized because of their apparent negative social impact (Samoff 2012; Ball and Youdell 2008; Klees 2012; Robertson et al. 2012). Even a former chief economist at the World Bank acknowledged that these programmes did not "promote the development of the poorest countries in the world":

No doubt, the Washington Consensus represented, in part, a reaction to the failures of the state in attempting to correct those of the market. But the pendulum swung too far in the other direction and for too long. (Stiglitz 2004: 3)

---

[13] The term was coined in 1989 by the English economist John Williamson.

[14] The prescriptions included policies in such areas as macroeconomic stabilization, economic opening with respect to both trade and investment, and the expansion of market forces within the domestic economy.

[15] SAPs consisted in the application of forms of conditionalities to developing countries, especially in Sub-Saharan Africa, to get new loans and for obtaining lower interest rates on existing loans. SAPs generally implement "free market" programs and policy. These programs include internal changes (notably privatization and deregulation) as well as external ones, especially the reduction of trade barriers.

4 A Changing Global Education Landscape: Growing... 79

Since the 1990s, the discourse of a market for education goods and services has also been reinforced by the World Trade Organization's (WTO) General Agreement on Trade in Services[16] (GATS). This agreement represents an influential mechanism to promote the education market, in that it opens national education systems up to international service providers (Ball and Youdell 2008; Rose 2003). The introduction of education into the frameworks of GATS has generated a new wave of political transformations in the field of education (Verger and Robertson 2012). The constitution of the GATS became a turning point in the development of the so-called Global Education Industry (Verger et al. 2016). "Education, a once relatively protected and decommodified sector, is being liberalised and transformed into a multi-billion dollar industry, powered by market-liberalising proponents in the developed economies" (Robertson 2002). The global arrangements that result from the spread of neo-liberalism pose questions with regard to the status of education as a public good and the threat of considering it as an industry regulated by the rules of global trade (Robertson 2002).

The term *Global Education Industry*, first used by James Tooley[17] in 1999 to refer to the expansion of private schooling in developing countries, has recently been adopted by numerous academics to describe a growing economic sector which involves the production, exchange and use of educational goods at a global level (Verger et al. 2016). The *Global Education Industry* field embraces a wide range of economic actors which include chains of for-profit private schools, big education corporations, consultancy firms, philanthropic foundations, and advocacy networks all of which are changing the ways and forms in which education is regulated, funded and delivered.

The increased involvement of corporate actors is spreading worldwide, particularly in developing countries where it has expanded in the form of low-fee private schools (Srivastava 2013, 2016; Walford 2011, 2015; Härmä 2011). Indeed, it should be noted that the greater number of

---

[16] The General Agreement on Trade in Services (GATS) is a treaty of the World Trade Organization (WTO) that entered into force in January 1995 as a result of the Uruguay Round negotiations. It followed the General Agreement on Tariffs and Trade.

[17] James Tooley is professor of education policy at the Newcastle University (United Kingdom). He is also a policy entrepreneur and served as a consultant at the World Bank.

80   **R. Locatelli**

enrolments in private institutions often does not correspond to higher standards of wealth but is primarily the result of the expansion of low-fee private schools often targeting poor and disadvantaged groups in low-income countries.

Moreover, the greater variety of actors has given rise to an increasing use of *public–private partnerships* (PPPs) as innovative forms of educational arrangements. Although the concept and practice of PPPs are not new (Ginsburg 2012), the recent use of "the term PPPs has been associated with a sharp resurgence of interest in, and participation of, new kinds of private actors in educational governance" (Robertson et al. 2012: 5). Moreover, the concept of *partnership* itself is not exempt from ambiguity (Ball 2007; Draxler 2012). While partnerships may apparently look neutral and normatively correct, it is argued that they may also lead to the erosion of the "public" in education and to a diminished role of the State (Robertson and Verger 2012). The inclusion of low-fee private schools in PPP frameworks has been adopted on a large scale in low-income countries. Among others, the case of Liberia is a case of PPP established by the government which also includes Bridge International Academies, a corporate actor known for funding low-fee private schools in other countries in sub-Saharan Africa and South Asia.

4.5.2   The Consequences of Marketization

As above illustrated, the concept of privatization appears to be increasingly linked to that of marketization, which favours a vision of education as an individual and consumable good, in contrast to a vision of education seen as a public good. The arguments against privatization and marketization have been widely discussed in literature (Verger et al. 2016; Ball 2007, 2012; Burch 2009; Robertson et al. 2012; Rizvi 2016; Srivastava 2016). Numerous academics and human rights researchers have expressed concerns regarding how appropriate a growing involvement of private actors and market arrangements in the education sector at different levels may be.

Some have deemed it as being in conflict with the recognition of education as a human right, which implies that the State should maintain the

4 A Changing Global Education Landscape: Growing... 81

primary responsibility for education financing, delivery, monitoring and regulation.[18] Related to these concerns are issues of equity and social justice, since market engagement might promote corporate or individual interests rather than public/societal benefits, leading to greater inequality and social stratification (Macpherson et al. 2014). The greater emphasis of market-based solutions of choice and competition may have the effect of undermining social cohesion "and its correlative bases of political power" (Mazawi 2013: 49). Indeed, "[c]orporatization redistributes economic control and cultural control from the public to private interests. These redistributions of power undermine public democracy, just social transformation and critical citizenship while exacerbating material and symbolic inequality" (Saltman 2009: 9–10). Marketization may result in the weakening of State action thus undermining public values or social cohesion and fostering fragmentation and loss of public institutions (Tomlinson 1986; Minow 2003).

The greater participation of new/non-traditional actors operating outside a formal education scenario, characterized by scarce public resources, has made the education sector potentially attractive to actors with commercial interests. As a result, critical issues regarding the influence of private, for-profit actors have also been identified in relation to privatization of the governance of education and to its commodification where schools are increasingly compelled to act as businesses and students as consumers. It is argued that the consumer orientation that characterizes marketization also has implications for the educational process where the focus appears to be moved from the core relationship between the teacher and the student to a number of factors less related to the educational process (Karlsen 2000). Concerns have also been raised regarding the effects of marketization, especially in low-income countries, on the working conditions and de-professionalization of teachers (Locatelli 2018). Neo-liberal market ideologies re-articulate what constitutes quality of education, narrowing it down to the measurement and comparison of student perfor-

---

[18] See in this respect the General Comment No. 13 on the Right to Education (Art. 13 of the Covenant of Economic Social and Cultural Rights): "it is clear that article 13 regards **States as having principal responsibility for the direct provision** of education in most circumstances; States parties recognize, for example, that the "development of a system of schools at all levels shall be actively pursued" (Art. 13 (2) (e))" (emphasis added).

82   R. Locatelli

mance in easily quantifiable academic features, particularly literacy and numeracy. Narrow approaches to education may push aside important social and equity concerns, compromising efforts of educational institutions to respond to social change, with potential risks for the reproduction of inequalities and for social stratification.

Moreover, profit engagement raises important issues with regard to the ultimate purposes of education. Although the provision of education may not be necessarily privatized, the commercial approach to education makes the *purposes* of education increasingly pending towards individual private interests (Lubienski 2003). Since the main concern of business actors is profit making, this may have repercussions on the social and civic objectives of education. As clearly argued by David Labaree (2011), the compromise between two different understandings of the purposes of education has always been difficult to reach, if not impossible:

> [w]e want schools to express our highest ideals as a society and our greatest aspirations as individuals, but only as long as they remain ineffective in actually enabling us to achieve these goals, since we really do not want to acknowledge that these two aims are at odds with each other. We ask schools to promote equality while preserving privilege, so we perpetuate a system that is too busy balancing opposites to promote student learning. We focus on making the system inclusive at one level and exclusive at the next, in order to make sure that it meets demands for both access and advantage. As a result, the system continues to lure us to pursue the dream of fixing society by reforming schools while continually frustrating our ability to meet these goals. It locks us in a spiral of educational expansion and credential inflation that has come to deplete our resources and exhaust our vitality. And we cannot find a simple cure for this syndrome because we will not accept any remedy that would mean giving up one of our aims for education in favor of another. We want it both ways. (p. 394)

With an exaggerated focus on school choice, the marketization of education becomes a question of "market mechanisms and consumer sovereignty—rather than public debate and explicit priorities over the big questions about the purposes and design of schooling" (Minow 2011:

845). Yet, at least in democratic societies, "there ought to be an ongoing discussion about the aims and ends of (public) education" (Biesta 2009: 37). This is particularly important given the multifaceted process of privatization, where the implications on political and socio-cultural dimensions are often undervalued.

Given the ever-increasing interconnection between different forms and practices in privatization policies, the multiplication of public and private actors involved in education, as well as the diversification of sources of financing, the principal difference between the definition of the public and the private in education is becoming less evident (Kitaev 1999; Ball 2007; Olmedo 2016). Moreover, the increase in the outsourcing of services, in the intervention of public institutions acting as enterprises in the market, and more generally in the interaction between the two sectors contribute to the blurring of boundaries between concepts of the public and the private (Ball 2007).

The consideration according to which public actors should promote the public interest and private ones should promote the private interest has also somehow collapsed since the State itself is directly involved in a process of privatization in education. Indeed, forms of privatization and of marketization are possible, thanks to the direct intervention of the State (Ball 2007). As argued by many scholars, the challenge is not merely an economic one, about the choice between the State and the market but an essential issue of democracy which concerns what government is for and for whom (Reich 2015; Rizvi 2016).

In this context, the notion of education as a public good becomes increasingly more difficult to define since the State is no longer identified with the "public" but is viewed as merely another economic actor among others (Rizvi 2016). This blurred vision may result in a lack of clarity in terms of roles and responsibilities among the different actors involved in education, with important consequences for the role of the State as the primary guarantor of education as a public good. However, if public and private actors are expected to continue interacting, what is needed is a qualitatively different understanding of *public* for the democratic governance of education.

References

Ashley, L. D., et al. (2014). *The Role and Impact of Private Schools in Developing Countries: A Rigorous Review of the Evidence*. Final Report (EPPI-Centre Education Rigorous Literature Review Reference Number 2206). London: Department for International Development. Retrieved from www.gov.uk/government/uploads/system/uploads/attachment_data/file/439702/private-schools-full-report.pdf.

Ball, S. J. (2007). *Education PLC*. London: Routledge.

Ball, S. J. (2012). *Global Education Inc*. London: Routledge.

Ball, S. J., & Youdell, D. (2008). *Hidden Privatisation in Public Education*. Brussels: Education International.

Belfield, C. R., & Levin, H. M. (2002). *Education Privatization: Causes, Consequences and Planning Implications* (Fundamentals of Educational Planning, 74). Paris: UNESCO International Institute for Educational Planning.

Bhatta, P., & Pherali, T. (2017). *Nepal: Patterns of Privatisation in Education: A Case Study of Low-Fee Private Schools and Private Chain Schools*. Brussels: Education International.

Biesta, G. J. J. (2009). Good Education in an Age of Measurement: On the Need to Reconnect with the Question of Purpose in Education. *Educational Assessment, Evaluation and Accountability, 21*(1), 33–46.

Burch, P. (2009). *Hidden Markets. The New Education Privatization*. London: Routledge.

Burchardt, T. (1997). *Boundaries Between Public and Private Welfare: A Typology and Map of Services*. CASE Paper 2. London: Centre for Analysis of Social Exclusion, London School of Economics.

Burchardt, T., Hills, J., & Propper, C. (1999). *Private Welfare and Public Policy*. York: Joseph Rowntree Foundation.

Carney, S. (2009). Negotiating Policy in an Age of Globalization: Exploring Educational "Policyscapes" in Denmark, Nepal, and China. *Comparative Education Review, 53*(1), 63–88.

Chubb, J. E., & Moe, T. M. (1990). *Politics, Markets and America's Schools*. Washington, DC: Brookings Institution.

Coomans, F., & Hallo de Wolf, A. (2005). Privatisation of Education and the Right to Education. In K. De Feyter & F. Gómez Isa (Eds.), *Privatisation and Human Rights in the Age of Globalisation* (pp. 229–258). Antwerp and Oxford: Intersentia.

4 A Changing Global Education Landscape: Growing... 85

Cucchiara, M., Gold, E., & Simon, E. (2011). Contracts, Choice, and Customer Service: Marketization and Public Engagement in Education. *Teachers College Record, 113*(11), 2460–2502.

Draxler, A. (2012). International PPPs in Education: New Potential or Privatizing Public Goods? In S. L. Robertson, K. Mundy, A. Verger, & F. Menashy (Eds.), *Public Private Partnerships in Education: New Actors and Modes of Governance in a Globalizing World* (pp. 43–62). Cheltenham: Edward Elgar.

Friedman, M. (1955). The Role of Government in Education. Retrieved from www.schoolchoices.org/roo/fried1.htm.

Friedman, M. (2002 [1962]). Capitalism and Freedom. Chicago, IL: University of Chicago Press.

Ginsburg, M. (2012). Public Private Partnerships, Neoliberal Globalization and Democratization. In S. L. Robertson, K. Mundy, A. Verger, & F. Menashy (Eds.), *Public Private Partnerships in Education: New Actors and Modes of Governance in a Globalizing World* (pp. 63–78). Cheltenham: Edward Elgar.

Härmä, J. (2011). *Lagos Private School Census 2010–2011 Report.* Abuja, Nigeria, Education Sector Support Programme in Nigeria, UK Department for International Development (Report, LG501).

Hood, C. (1991). A Public Management for All Seasons? *Public Administration Review, 69*(Spring), 3–19.

Karlsen, G. E. (2000). Decentralized Centralism: Framework for a Better Understanding of Governance in the Field of Education. *Journal of Education Policy, 15*(5), 525–538.

Kitaev, I. (1999). *Private Education in Sub-Saharan Africa: A Re-Examination of Theories and Concepts Related to Its Development and Finance* (Mechanisms and Strategies of Educational Finance). Paris: UNESCO International Institute for Educational Planning.

Kitaev, I. (2001). Privatisation de l'éducation: un débat d'actualité. *Lettre d'information de l'IIPE.* XIX, 1. Paris: UNESCO International Institute for Educational Planning.

Klees, S. (2012). World Bank and Education: Ideological Premises and Ideological Conclusions. In S. Klees, J. Samoff, & N. P. Stromquist (Eds.), *The World Bank and Education: Critiques and Alternatives* (pp. 49–65). Rotterdam: Sense Publishers.

Klees, S., Samoff, J., & Stromquist, N. P. (Eds.). (2012). *The World Bank and Education: Critiques and Alternatives.* Rotterdam: Sense Publishers.

Labaree, D. F. (2011). Consuming the Public School. *Educational Theory, 61*(4), 381–394.

LaRocque, N. (2008). Public-Private Partnerships in Basic Education: An International Review. *Literature Review*. CfBT Education Trust.

Laval, C. (2003). *L'école n'est pas une entreprise: Le néo-libéralisme à l'assaut de l'enseignement public*. Paris: Editions la Découverte.

Lewis, L., & Patrinos, H. A. (2012). *Impact Evaluation of Private Sector Participation in Education*. Research Report. The World Bank and CfBT Education Trust.

Locatelli, R. (2018). *The Implications of Education Privatization on Teachers in Lower-Income Countries*. Background Paper for the 13th Session of the Joint ILO–UNESCO Committee of Experts on the Application of the Recommendations Concerning Teaching Personnel (CEART). Paris: UNESCO; Geneva: International Labour Organization.

Lubienski, C. (2003). Instrumentalist Perspectives on the "Public" in Public Education: Incentives and Purposes. *Educational Policy, 17*(4), 478–502.

Macpherson, I., Robertson, S. L., & Walford, G. (2014). *Education, Privatization and Social Justice: Case Studies from Africa, South Asia and South East Asia*. Oxford: Symposium Books.

Mazawi, A. E. (2013). Grammars of Privatization, Schooling, and the "Network State". In T. Szkudlarek (Ed.), *Education and the Political*. Rotterdam: Sense Publishers.

Minow, M. (2003). Public and Private Partnerships: Accounting for the New Religion. *Harvard Law Review, 116*(5), 1229–1270.

Minow, M. (2011). Confronting the Seduction of Choice: Law, Education, and American Pluralism. *The Yale Law Journal, 120*, 814–848.

Moumné, R., & Saudemont, C. (2015). *Overview of the Role of the Role of Private Providers in Education in Light of the Existing International Legal Framework. Investments in Private Education: Undermining or Contributing to the Full Development of the Human Right to Education?* UNESCO Working Papers on Education Policy, 1. Paris: UNESCO.

National Population Commission (Nigeria) and ORC Macro. (2004). *Nigeria DHS EdData Survey 2004: Education Data for Decision-Making*. Calverton, MD: National Population Commission and ORC Macro.

National Population Commission (Nigeria) and RTI International. (2016). *2015 Nigeria Education Data Survey (NEDS)*. Washington, DC: United States Agency for International Development.

Noddings, N. (2005). *The Challenge to Care in Schools: An Alternative Approach to Education* (2nd ed.). New York: Teacher's College Press.

4 A Changing Global Education Landscape: Growing… 87

OECD. (2004). *OECD Handbook for Internationally Comparative Education Statistics Concepts, Standards, Definitions and Classifications*. Paris: Organisation for Economic Co-operation and Development.

Olmedo, A. (2016). Philanthropic Governance: Charitable Companies, the Commercialization of Education and That Thing Called "Democracy". In A. Verger, C. Lubienski, & G. Steiner-Khamsi (Eds.), *The Global Education Industry. World Yearbook of Education 2016* (pp. 44–62). London: Routledge.

Orbach, B. (2013). What Is Government Failure. *Yale Journal on Regulation Online, 30*, 44–56.

Pedró, F., Leroux, G., & Watanabe, M. (2015). *The Privatization of Education in Developing Countries: Evidence and Policy Implications*. UNESCO Working Papers on Education Policy, 2. Paris: UNESCO.

Reich, R. (2015). *Saving Capitalism: For the Many, Not the Few*. New York: Alfred Knopf.

Reid, A. (2012). Federalism, Public Education and the Public Good. In *Perspectives*. Sydney: The Whitlam Institute.

Rizvi, F. (2016). *Privatization in Education: Trends and Consequences*. ERF Working Papers Series, 18. Paris: UNESCO.

Rizvi, F., & Lingard, B. (2010). *Globalizing Education Policy*. London: Routledge.

Robertson, S. L. (2002). WTO/Gats and the Global Education Services Industry. *Globalisation, Societies and Education, 1*(3), 259–266.

Robertson, S. L., Mundy, K., Verger, A., & Menashy, F. (2012). An Introduction to Public Private Partnerships and Education Governance. In S. L. Robertson, K. Mundy, A. Verger, & F. Menashy (Eds.), *Public Private Partnerships in Education: New Actors and Modes of Governance in a Globalizing World* (pp. 1–17). Cheltenham: Edward Elgar.

Robertson, S. L., & Verger, A. (2012). Governing Education Through Public Private Partnerships. In S. L. Robertson, K. Mundy, A. Verger, & F. Menashy (Eds.), *Public Private Partnerships in Education: New Actors and Modes of Governance in a Globalizing World* (pp. 21–42). Cheltenham: Edward Elgar.

Rolleston, C., & Adefeso-Olateju, M. (2014). De Facto Privatisation of Basic Education in Africa: A Market Response to Government Failure? A Comparative Study of the Cases of Ghana and Nigeria. In I. Macpherson, S. L. Robertson, & G. Walford (Eds.), *Education, Privatization and Social Justice: Case Studies from Africa, South Asia and South East Asia* (pp. 25–44). Oxford: Symposium Books.

Rose, P. (2003). From the Washington to the Post-Washington Consensus: The Influence of International Agendas on Education Policy and Practice in Malawi. *Globalisation, Societies and Education, 1*(1), 67–86.

Saltman, K. J. (2009). Putting the Public Back in Public Schooling: Public Schools Beyond the Corporate Model. *DePaul Journal for Social Justice, 3*(1), 9–39.

Samoff, J. (2012). More of the Same Will Not Do. Learning Without Learning in the World Bank's 2020 Education Strategy. In S. Klees, J. Samoff, & N. P. Stromquist (Eds.), *The World Bank and Education: Critiques and Alternatives* (pp. 109–121). Rotterdam: Sense Publishers.

Scott, J., & DiMartino, C. (2009). Public Education Under New Management: A Typology of Educational Privatization Applied to New York City's Restructuring. *Peabody Journal of Education, 84*, 432–452.

Srivastava, P. (2013). Low-Fee Private Schooling: Issues and Evidence. In P. Srivastava (Ed.), *Low-Fee Private Schooling Aggravating Equity or Mitigating Disadvantage?* (pp. 7–35). Oxford: Symposium Books.

Srivastava, P. (2016). Questioning the Global Scaling Up of Low-Fee Private Schooling: The Nexus Between Business, Philanthropy, and PPPs. In A. Verger, C. Lubienski, & G. Steiner-Khamsi (Eds.), *The Global Education Industry. World Yearbook of Education 2016* (pp. 248–263). London: Routledge.

Starr, P. (1988). The Meaning of Privatization. *Yale Law and Policy Review, 6*, 6–41.

Stiglitz, J. E. (2004). *The Post Washington Consensus Consensus*. The Initiative for Policy Dialogue.

Tomlinson, J. (1986). Public Education, Public Good. *Oxford Review of Education, 12*(3), 211–222.

Tooley, J. (1999). *The Global Education Industry: Lessons from Private Education in Developing Countries*. London: Institute of Economic Affairs.

UIS. (2016). *Instruction Manual: Survey of Formal Education*. Montreal: UNESCO Institute for Statistics.

UIS and IIEP. (2016). *Who Pays for What in Education? The Real Costs Revealed Through National Education Accounts*. Montreal: UNESCO Institute for Statistics.

UIS and UNESCO. (2016, July). *Leaving No One Behind: How Far on the Way to Universal Primary and Secondary Education?* Policy Paper 27/Fact Sheet 37. Paris: UNESCO.

UNCTAD. (2015). *World Investment Report 2015: Reforming International Investment Governance*. Geneva: United Nations Conference on Trade and Development.

UNESCO. (2014). *Teaching and Learning: Achieving Quality for All*. EFA Global Monitoring Report 2013/4. Paris: UNESCO.

4 A Changing Global Education Landscape: Growing...   89

UNESCO. (2015a). *Rethinking Education: Towards a Global Common Good?* Paris: UNESCO.

UNESCO. (2015b). *Education for All 2000–2015—Achievements and Challenges*. EFA Global Monitoring Report 2015. Paris: UNESCO.

UNESCO. (2016). *Education for People and Planet: Creating Sustainable Futures for All*. Global Education Monitoring Report 2016. Paris: UNESCO.

Verger, A. (2012). Framing and Selling Global Education Policy: The Promotion of Public–Private Partnerships for Education in Low-Income Contexts. *Journal of Education Policy, 27*(1), 109–130.

Verger, A., Lubienski, C., & Steiner-Khamsi, G. (2016). The Emergence and Structuring of the Global Education Industry: Towards an Analytical Framework. In A. Verger, C. Lubienski, & G. Steiner-Khamsi (Eds.), *The Global Education Industry. World Yearbook of Education 2016* (pp. 3–24). London: Routledge.

Verger, A., & Robertson, S. L. (2012). The GATS Game-Changer: International Trade Regulation and the Constitution of a Global Education Marketplace. In S. L. Robertson, K. Mundy, A. Verger, & F. Menashy (Eds.), *Public Private Partnerships in Education: New Actors and Modes of Governance in a Globalizing World* (pp. 104–127). Cheltenham: Edward Elgar.

Vinokur, A. (2004). Public, privé,... ou hybride ? *Cahiers de la recherche sur l'éducation et les savoirs, 3*, 13–33.

Viteri, F. (2016). *Spatial Mapping for Improved Intra-Urban Education Planning*. Background Paper for UNESCO Global Education Monitoring Report 2016.

Walford, G. (2011). Low-Fee Private Schools in England and in Less Economically Developed Countries: What Can We Learn from a Comparison? *Compare, 41*(3), 401–413.

Walford, G. (2015). The Globalisation of Low-Fee Private Schools. In J. Zajda (Ed.), *Second International Handbook on Globalisation, Education and Policy Research* (pp. 309–320). Dordrecht: Springer.

Wells, A. S., & Scott, J. (2001). Privatization and Charter Schools: Political, Economic and Social Dimensions. In H. M. Levin (Ed.), *Privatizing Education: Can the Marketplace Deliver Equity, Efficiency, Choice, and Social Cohesion?* (pp. 234–257). New York: Westview.

Whitty, G., & Power, S. (2000). Marketization and Privatization in Mass Education Systems. *International Journal of Educational Development, 20*, 93–107.

Wodon, Q. (2014). *Education in Sub-Saharan Africa: Comparing Faith-Inspired, Private Secular, and Public Schools*. Washington, DC: World Bank.

5

Reframing the Concept of Education As a Public Good

This chapter deals with developing a systematic organization of two different approaches to education, one that puts greater emphasis on the public-goods and the other on the private-goods aspects of education. The chapter outlines the policy implications with regard to the various functions of the State by taking into account different combinations of higher and lower levels of democracy and of privatization and develops a quadrant which synthetizes these two interrelated dimensions. The analysis gives an insight into how the role of the State can be reinterpreted in the light of the changing education landscape. It further identifies "criteria of publicness" that refer to both formal and functional conditions: the former related to the democratic governance of education systems and the latter to the development of democratic pedagogy and curricula. These criteria should be valid for all institutions and actors, irrespectively of their public or private nature. This chapter finally draws on the research by Gert Biesta (2012) who frames the theoretical debate on education in the public sphere. However, since processes of marketization pose not only an economic challenge but also a political one, about the democratic functioning of institutions, it is suggested that the way the public sphere should be reconstituted requires a radical change in the approach to education policy and practices.

© The Author(s) 2019
R. Locatelli, *Reframing Education as a Public and Common Good*,
https://doi.org/10.1007/978-3-030-24801-7_5

5.1 In Search of a Balance Between Two Contrasting Approaches to Education

A substantial degree of ambiguity exists in the way that education is perceived as a private or public good. The way this issue is addressed has serious implications for the control and governance of education. As illustrated in Chap. 3, according to the economic classification of goods, education is commonly considered an impure public good and is provided in a hybrid public–private model (Lubienski 2003). Indeed, education is a particular kind of good which exhibits both public and private aspects. The effects produced by education are both individual and general and therefore justify personal and collective claims on its governance. Indeed, not only do individuals have private benefits from being educated but, at the same time, thanks to its positive externalities (or "neighbours effect"), education is considered as having public-good aspects as well: the provision of mass schooling is thought to be evident in indicators such as civic cohesion and crime rates, and for these reasons it is worthy of public debate and policy-making. This two-fold classification of education, characterized by both public-good and private-good aspects, is also acknowledged by Levin (2000) who describes the "peculiar nature of education" as follows:

> Embedded in the same educational experience are outcomes that can contribute to the overall society as well as those which can provide private gains to the individual. (2000: 3)

In this respect, the idea that private interests are antithetical to the "public good" raises challenges, because educational outcomes serve private as well as public interests—and in many ways, these outcomes are inextricably linked through gains in the productivity and civic efficacy of the individual learner (Levin 2000).

Schooling is the major mechanism for setting up a society that is educated to understand, accept and function within a universally accepted set of institutional principles. A smoothly functioning society means that all, or most, of its members accept a shared understanding of the values

5 Reframing the Concept of Education As a Public Good

and principles that underlie the legal, political, social and economic foundations that constitute the society. Much of the educational process is oriented towards creating for all children and young people a common experience that enables them to understand these institutions and prepares them for effective participation. This is the reason for the universal aim of "education for democracy" (Levin 2010). In short, a major function of the system of schooling is to reproduce the most basic functions and institutions of society from generation to generation through common socialization. Moreover, in democratic societies schools are considered the major institutions responsible for giving all young people a fair chance in life. This mission entails adopting various approaches to the creation of equity in the allocation of resources and educational outcomes in order to compensate for initial economic differences among children. Indeed, equity is one of the underlying principles in an approach to education seen as a public good. It "refers to the quest for fairness in access to educational opportunities, resources, and outcomes, by gender, social class, race, language origins, disability, and geographical location of students" (Levin 2010). This is also essential to ensure that education is socially just. Given these public-good aspects, the State is considered as having a predominant role in the governance of education in order to ensure that principles of equity and social justice are respected.

However, recent trends in privatization and marketization of education, characterized by policies promoting deregulation and liberalization within the system, economically based competition, as well as the emergence of private suppliers of education services, tend to give greater prominence to the private-good aspects of education. As argued by Macpherson et al. (2014):

> Education as development thus essentially followed the same dual objectives—making citizens and making economies—as had informed the growth of Europe in the nineteenth and twentieth centuries. These two very different understandings of 'education' in education policy, the one broadly humanitarian, the other deeply economic, were to become the basis of a division that has persisted across the decades since, but where since the 1990s, a strong reframing of education by economists has become hegemonic, in part a result of processes broadly conceived of as 'globalisation'. (p. 12)

Private benefits include those that are conferred on and limited to the individuals being educated and their families. Families usually favour specific approaches to the education of their children, and they prefer schools that reflect similar perspectives and ideals. Students who receive more and better schooling benefit from greater understanding of themselves and their society and are able to convert their skills into higher incomes, more satisfying jobs, favourable personal contacts, better health and greater political and social understanding (Levin 2010). These private benefits can be substantial for both educated individuals and their families. In this perspective, for the individual and the family, the solution is for the system to provide a diversity of educational choices, encouraging schools to match as closely as possible their private aspirations and capabilities. Freedom of choice puts greater emphasis on the private benefits of education and the liberty to ensure that families choose schools that are consistent with their parental ideas. Moreover, emphasis is placed on the greater efficiency of some schools in obtaining better educational results than others. The efficiency frame rests on the acceptance of poor governance and weak institutions, with the State deemed as incapable of maximizing resources. In contrast, the private sector is considered to be more efficient and therefore better able to regulate these deficiencies. Indeed, advocates of choice believe that competition among schools will increase productive efficiency (Levin 2010).

These two different approaches to education, one that puts greater emphasis on the public-good and the other on private-good aspects of education, could be summarized as shown in Table 5.1.

If education is perceived as a private good, then markets are considered as offering the most appropriate model for production and distribution. Indeed, private goods typically involve benefits that accrue primarily to individuals and are therefore left to private control, exercised through market mechanisms. The promise of personal gain has been a driving force in the popular demand for education as a private good. Therefore, an individual seeking an education in order to translate that credential into socioeconomic rewards should have some significant degree of control over the type of education provided (Lubienski 2003). With this in mind, it can be said that marketization tends to give far greater prominence to the private-good aspects of education. Effects of marketization

5 Reframing the Concept of Education As a Public Good

Table 5.1 Public-good versus market-based approach

	Public-good approach	Market-based approach
Aim	Basic quality education for all	Measureable learning
Purposes of education	Public/societal benefits	Individual/corporate benefits
Function	"Education for democracy"	Education for competitiveness
Perspective	Students as "citizens"	Students as "consumers"
Dimension	Socio-political	Economic and technical
Values	Equity, social justice, equality	Efficiency, freedom of choice
Vision	Humanistic	Utilitarian/human capital
Governance	Primary responsibility of the State	Residual role of the State

are seen not just in the emergence of different structures but also in the shift of power to narrower segments of society defined by individual private interests. It is argued that this shift has political implications, leading to the weakening of the role of the State in the governance of education and to a reduction of the public-good aspects of education, making it excludable and rivalrous, thus diminishing broader forms of public control over schooling.

5.2 Revisiting the Role of the State

As previously illustrated, considering education as a public good implies that the State maintains some form of intervention in the educational process in order to ensure at least basic quality education for all. Indeed, the concept of education as a public good is based on both economic as well as political considerations. From an economic perspective, the benefits of education extend beyond the individual and this requires some sort of intervention on the part of the State. Moreover, according to political arguments, which focus on the institutional regulation of goods, the State continues to play an indispensable role as the ultimate guarantor of the public sphere, where democratic processes can be fulfilled. However, concrete implications of the principle of education as a public good with regard to the role of the State vary considerably depending on contexts.

First and foremost, it is necessary to determine whether a public-good approach is possible in non-democratic societies. If that is the case, what are the minimal conditions for the role of the State within such an approach? What if the State is the only actor in policy formulation, funding, delivery, monitoring and regulation of education? Is it possible to adopt a public-good approach within authoritarian regimes? Inevitably, the implications of the concept of education as a public good vary according to the level of democracy or to the political regimes.

5.2.1 Defining the Role of the State

It can be argued that a public-good approach may have different implications for countries according to the level of democracy of a specific context and to the range of involvement of non-state actors. For instance, in some non-democratic countries, the State is predominantly the only actor which provides, funds, regulates and monitors the system. Education can be considered as a public good as long as the State officially fulfils these functions and adopts and implements education policies which represent minimal conditions for ensuring that all children have access to free education and that an education system is put in place. However, it should be underlined that an approach to education seen as a public good also aims to achieve *quality* education for all. This condition would hardly be realized in such contexts where an effective democratic functioning is challenged or completely non-existent and where voices other than the State are not heard. In such contexts, however, equity concerns could somehow be addressed if the State ensures that education is provided *for all*. Still, this would not include *quality* considerations, which require the system to be democratic within an integrated approach to education.

Moreover, even within systems that are democratic, at least officially, the role of the State is changing due to the greater involvement of private actors at all levels of the education endeavour. As illustrated in previous chapters, private actors are increasingly involved in the provision, funding, monitoring and policy-making of education. Therefore, in the light of this changing context, what are the implications of the concept of education as a public good for the role of the State? What should be

5 Reframing the Concept of Education As a Public Good 97

expected from the State in order to achieve free quality education for all? Is it about the key role of the State in policy formulation, financing, delivery, monitoring, regulation? Or are some of these functions more central than others within an approach to education seen as a public good?

Figure 5.1 represents the role of the State according to combinations of lower and higher levels of democracy and involvement of private actors in different political regimes.

As already mentioned, the concept of education as a public good implies that the State guarantees free quality education for all, at least during the compulsory years. This represents the underlying principle

Socio-democratic welfare states		Liberal democratic systems
Primary role of the State in ensuring free quality basic education for all. Funding, provision, monitoring, and regulation of the system. The State has a crucial role in direct provision and funding of quality educational opportunities.	Level of democracy - HIGH	Primary role of the State in the *regulation* and *monitoring* of the system in order to guarantee free quality basic education for all, given the greater variety of actors involved. States also need ensure minimum levels of funding and provision in order to protect equity and quality education for all.
LOW - Level of private involvement		Level of private involvement-**HIGH**
Non-democratic regimes		**Weak democratic systems**
Primary (often unique) role of the State in ensuring free basic education for *all* through funding, provision, monitoring, regulation of the system. Criticism: difficulties of achieving *quality* education for all, giving the lack of a full democratic functioning system	LOW - Level of democracy	Need to strengthen the different functions of the State, above all the *regulatory and monitoring* function given the increasing involvement of non-state actors. The role of the State is also fundamental with regard to *funding* and *provision*. Criticism: At the same time, need to strengthen the functioning of democratic institutions in order to achieve *quality* education.

Fig. 5.1 Role of the State according to combinations of lower and higher levels of democracy and of private actors' involvement

assumed by international organizations such as United Nations Educational, Scientific and Cultural Organization (UNESCO) and by human rights activists, researchers and academics. As envisaged in the Incheon Declaration and Framework for Action, adopted in 2015 at the World Education Forum (Incheon, Republic of Korea), States are committed to "increase public spending on education in accordance with country context, and urge adherence to the international and regional benchmarks of allocating efficiently at least 4–6% of Gross Domestic Product and/or at least 15–20% of total public expenditure to education" (UNESCO 2015). The Framework for Action affirms that "Governments have the primary responsibility to deliver on the right to education, and a central role as custodians of efficient, equitable and effective management and financing of public education" (UNESCO 2015: 78). The Education Commission also compels States to mobilize more domestic resources for education and to improve funding mechanisms through increased tax revenues and resource reallocation (Education Commission 2016).

The State should be the ultimate guarantor of the education system in order to avoid the risk of privatization and marketization generating inequalities and social stratification. Not only is this position prevalent among the research and academic community but has also been acknowledged in a policy paper by economists of the International Monetary Fund (IMF) (Ostry et al. 2016). Indeed, it is stated that "the IMF recognizes that full capital flow liberalization is not always an appropriate end-goal, and that further liberalization is more beneficial and less risky if countries have reached certain thresholds of financial and institutional development". Increased spending on education and training is considered as an appropriate "predistribution policy", suitable for mitigating some impacts of the economic damage coming from inequality. Of course, the perspective adopted by the IMF on issues of inequality is based on an economic rationale that considers the adverse effects that inequality would have on the level and durability of growth. Nevertheless, it is important to underline at this point that concepts of neo-liberalism are evolving, and even within the IMF, there are concerns that a reduced involvement of the State may give rise to inequalities.

5 Reframing the Concept of Education As a Public Good   99

Having said this, it should be emphasized that given the expanding demand for education at all levels and the need to ensure *free* and *quality* education, States cannot always be self-sufficient in the funding and management of the education system (Rizvi 2016).The current situation however presents the serious risk that easy-to-consume, replicable and marketable solutions may take the upper hand over more elaborate and sophisticated mechanisms of reform that may require a much deeper understanding of the historical, anthropological and cultural conditions that characterize a specific educational context and that therefore call for a revision of the aims and of the ways these institutions function. It is argued that, given private-sector development, market arrangements may diminish the role of the State with regard to its functions as financer, manager and regulator. In line with this, Roger Wettenhall (2003) identifies five main roles involved in the management of public affairs that refer to producer, owner, provider, regulator and facilitator. He argues that each of them "could be performed by either the state, the market or civil society, and that many different state/market/civil society combinations are possible" (p. 82). The above authors warn against the dangerous impact to the public interest with regard to the diminished or displaced role of the State within these new arrangements.

5.2.2 Beyond Funding and Provision, to Regulation and Monitoring

Over and above the need to ensure minimum conditions in terms of funding, as envisaged by the Incheon Declaration and in the Framework for Action, new and innovative financial mechanisms need to be identified (UNESCO 2015; Education Commission 2016). A more detailed discussion on the necessity and ways in which States could be supported in the development of education systems will be dealt with later. For now, it is important to underline what should be the role of the State with regard to the changing educational landscape, characterized by greater private involvement. Indeed, the State should maintain an important function with regard to the *funding* and *provision* of education opportunities. This is even more important in those contexts where inequality is

100   R. Locatelli

staggering and calls for a greater intervention especially in those areas where children are more at risk of exclusion or discrimination. In this respect, international cooperation in education should also support States to develop a public education system in order to ensure free and quality basic education for all. At the same time, and perhaps even more importantly nowadays, the role of the State should be strengthened particularly with regard to its *regulatory* and *monitoring* functions, which are more and more fundamental in a context of greater participation of private actors at all levels of the education endeavour. Indeed, as remarked by Walford (2001):

> Privatisation cannot be labelled "good" or "bad" … What is important is the ways in which the state and others have acted to structure the privatisation process and the ways in which schools can subsequently operate. (p. 179)

In this perspective, the principle of education as a public good implies that the State strengthens above all its *regulatory* function, especially at the basic and compulsory level, in order to guarantee the conditions under which *free* and *quality* education for all can be ensured. While in "richer countries, governments have entered into elaborate funding and monitoring arrangements with private actors … in poorer countries, the private sector is loosely regulated" (UNESCO 2016: 145). The need for greater state regulation is at the centre of the recently adopted Abidjan Principles which aim to develop a normative framework to assess privatization from a social justice perspective. In particular, Principle 4 encourages *all* States to "take all effective measures, including particularly the adoption and enforcement of effective regulatory measures, to ensure the realisation of the right to education where private actors are involved in the provision of education".[1]

It is increasingly important in the current context that the State guarantees the opportunities of quality education for all and at the same time

---

[1] Principle 4 of the *Guiding Principles on the human rights obligations of States to provide public education and to regulate private involvement in education* (the Abidjan Principles), available at this link: https://static1.squarespace.com/static/5c2d081daf2096648cc801da/t/5c98f18eeef1a11d127a28d6/1553527205168/Abidjan-Principles-EN.pdf.

5 Reframing the Concept of Education As a Public Good 101

assures the principles that should inspire the whole education policy. The nature of the public may be reinterpreted, in that the primary responsibility of the State is to strengthen and guarantee the framework in which education is provided. This framework should be inspired by principles of equity, equality of opportunities, social cohesion, social justice and human rights. At the same time, the State needs to ensure that a diversified educational offer is available, in order to guarantee freedom of choice, which would be grounded on the principle of "diversity" rather than competition. As argued by Whitty and Power (2000):

> We need to ask how we can use the positive aspects of choice and autonomy to facilitate the development of new forms of community empowerment rather than exacerbating social differentiation. (p. 105)

This regulatory function is essential for ensuring that education is considered as a public good and should therefore be carefully developed and implemented. However, it should not be limited to merely preserving the institutional framework for the operation of private actors, providing regulations simply on curriculum objectives, completion, admission tests, health and safety (Heyneman and Stern 2014). While ensuring some levels of flexibility and autonomy, the State should also regulate teacher certification and pedagogy as well as school fees and define curriculum standards and quality assurance mechanisms in order to guarantee both equity and quality in education. Together with the strengthening of the State's *regulatory* function is the need to ensure that a *monitoring* mechanism is implemented in a consultative and inclusive process ensuring transparency and accountability. Indeed, public authorities are increasingly required to be accountable to a democratically accountable government (Ranson 2008).

Taking into account the contribution by Bergan et al. (2009), Table 5.2 aims to provide a synthetic presentation of how the role of the State could be represented in a context characterized by greater involvement of non-state actors.

It should be noted that the above table may be valid only for levels of compulsory education since the role of the State varies depending on different levels of education.

102   R. Locatelli

Table 5.2 Roles and levels of responsibility of the State in education

Type of role	Level of responsibility	Description of the role
Regulation	Exclusive responsibility	Ensuring the framework of education, including the structure, the institutional framework, the framework of quality assurance and authoritative information To implement efficient mechanisms to compensate for differences, particularly important in countries experiencing powerful social imbalances This function cannot be left to others
Monitoring	Main responsibility	Devise and implement mechanisms for the evaluation of results obtained in the pursuit of those objectives, allowing a progressive degree of autonomy to institutions and local bodies in deciding by which methods these results are to be obtained
Policy-making	Main responsibility	To determine objectives and priorities through mechanisms of democratic discussion
Provision	Important responsibility	Public authorities should be heavily involved in the actual running of educational institutions and programmes, to contribute to good educational opportunities at reasonable conditions
Funding	Important responsibility	Public funds can and should be supplemented by money from other sources, but these alternative funding sources should never be a pretext for public authorities not to provide substantial public resources

Adapted from: Bergan et al. (2009)

Despite the growing trends of education privatization, the State maintains a fundamental role in achieving *free* and *quality* education for all, especially in the light of the increasing diversity of the stakeholders involved. Indeed, it is the guarantor of the right to education as foreseen in numerous conventions and declarations and in the Education 2030 agenda. As such, the State is the only actor that can ensure that due account is taken of the general interest and of the long-term vision. In the field of education, there is a need for more State but of a different quality. As already argued by Tedesco (1995) two decades ago, the State

5 Reframing the Concept of Education As a Public Good

cannot [...] fulfil this role by resorting to the same mechanisms as in the past, that is to say, by assuming the main responsibility for defining policies and implementing them. In this new context, the strategic role of the State should be to organize consultation, to place all of the necessary information on the discussion table, to evaluate results, to act wherever necessary and to guarantee respect for rules of the game that are accepted by all. (p. 109)

This different quality not only concerns the strengthening of some important functions relating to the regulation and monitoring of education systems but it also has to do with the nature of public institutions themselves. Indeed, it is necessary to understand which rules are being implemented and which norms, values and systems of power these rules reflect (Reich 2015). Given the blurring of boundaries between the public and the private and the ongoing processes of privatization, it is important to define what can be considered as *public* in education.

5.3 What Is It That Makes Education a *Public* Good?

As previously illustrated, the distinction between public and private in education is increasingly blurred as public actors interact more and more frequently with non-state actors. This is acknowledged in the greater involvement of households in the funding of educational opportunities for their children or in the higher complementation of public and private arrangements at all levels of education. Moreover, the consideration according to which public actors should promote the public interest and private ones should promote the private interest has somehow collapsed since the State itself is directly involved in a process of privatization in education, wherein public actors themselves act as corporate/business organizations implementing education policies that put greater emphasis on individual achievement and progress, in contrast to a vision of education which first and foremost should produce public benefits. In this respect, it should be underlined that forms of privatization and of marketization are possible also thanks to the direct intervention of the State.

104   R. Locatelli

Indeed, "neoliberalism has succeeded in changing the connection between politics and economy in much of the world. (...) [I]t has dismantled the Keynesian welfare state, the system of regulated capitalism and state-supplied services that were dominant in the generation from 1945 to 1980. In the global periphery, neoliberalism has dismantled the social-democratic developmentalist state, and broken up the social alliances around it" (Connell 2013: 281).[2] It has been argued that the State is a "key ally in market-making processes" since its role is necessary in the creation of a space in which markets can prosper. States can promote pro-market regulation in different spheres (Verger et al. 2016: 13). In this respect, it is not possible to account for the disappearance of currently existing neo-liberalism without also addressing changes to the form and modalities of the State (Ball 2012).

It has been argued that the changing relations between state and non-state actors should be considered "as a new chapter in a long-running story of shifting relationships connecting public and private institutions, functions and identities. New shifts should be subject to overarching public rules and goals governing their development. In this light, public and private institutions can and should be viewed as partners, serving larger and multiple public ends" (Minow 2003: 1236). The involvement of non-state actors should be framed according to the notion of education as a public good, which implies that all actors are committed, within their own possibilities, to the democratic governance of education in order to foster the implementation of quality educational practices and methodologies that take into consideration the social and cultural diversity of different contexts.

Given that both public and private actors are called to contribute to the commitment to quality education for all, today more than ever, it is essential to identify what constitutes the "public" in education and how governance arrangements should operate according to this vision. As it has been affirmed, "[i]t may be more useful to consider what constitutes the publicness of schooling: how different aspects of schools align with public and private goods and interests and how those alignments are changing" (Lubienski 2003: 499). Since marketization poses not only an

---

[2] The developmentalist (or developmental) State is characterized by having strong state intervention, as well as extensive regulation and planning.

economic challenge but also one of democracy, the perspective that should be adopted takes into consideration both economic and political factors. Indeed, critical studies of education policy and markets raise serious questions about who benefits, who bears the burden of the cost, how these patterns are rooted in societal and political factors, and at what cost to democracy (Burch 2009). This is particularly important when education is considered as a public good since, as illustrated in Chap. 3, beyond economic factors related to economic theory, political considerations play an important role in the choice of solutions to the problem of public goods. A political perspective, therefore, enables us to identify the governance arrangements that are determinant for the achievement of the aims of a public goods approach and gives more clarity with regard to the nature and role of the State in the complex governance of education systems which involve both public and private actors.

The following sections identify the criteria on which the principle of education as a *public* good can be based. As illustrated by Higgins and Knight Abowitz (2011), not only do these criteria refer to "formal" factors such as access and governance but also take into account "functionalist" considerations that refer to the nature of pedagogy and of curriculum. This has strong political implications and is essential to identifying the nature of the State and its role at all levels of the education endeavour in different contexts. In this way, the concept of education as a public good takes the shape of a political project and a principle of governance which defines both the way in which education is organized and the purposes of the education system itself.

5.3.1 Formal Conditions

First and foremost, the concept of education as a public good would enhance the development of a democratic system of governance that the State needs to guarantee. Indeed, the notions of *public* and of *democracy* have been considered as being highly interconnected; "Democracy, as the power of those who have no qualification for exercising power, rests on the notion of the common as a space in which the equality for all gets continuously verified in the face of the unequal conditions of living that

106   R. Locatelli

constitute the wrong of this tension. (…) The privileged space for this to happen is in the common space of the public", a space, where all actors are represented and that should be ultimately guaranteed by the State (Rancière 2004, cited in Friedrich 2016: 161).

In this respect, it should be noted that just as neo-liberal policies create more space for market principles, they can reduce the space "for democratic processes in education policy and policies informed by public interest" (Burch 2009: 14). Ideologies of neo-liberalism have made education policy fit the requirements of the market. The private sector, which mainly consists in businesses grounded in an "audit culture", accommodates sectorial interests and is "appropriately termed 'corporate' to capture this separate, organizational and financial entity, interest and accountability" (Ranson 2008). As argued by Ranson,

> this neo-liberal regime of consumer choice and corporate control was designed, purportedly, to restore public trust by making services accountable and responsible to public choice conceived as consumer preference. Providing consumers with accounts of performance and service quality produced a regime of performativity that works from the outside in, through regulations, controls and pressures, but also from the inside out, colonizing lives and producing new subjectivities. […] Such a regime cannot realize its purposes of enhancing institutional achievement or strengthening public trust. (2008: 191–192)

The State therefore plays a fundamental role in ensuring that an effective democratic process is accomplished and that all actors take part in this process to an equal degree, by establishing the rules of operation of the education system and by ascertaining that they are transparent and respected by all actors. In this regard, the State should be democratic in its own way of functioning, allowing different stakeholders to have a say in the decision-making process. It is widely acknowledged that citizens, parents, parties and local representatives ask for more openness, more transparency and more involvement in the running of the institutions they finance (Caillods 1997). Within an approach to education as a public good, the democratic governance should be reflected at all levels of the educational endeavour, starting from the decision-making process up to

5 Reframing the Concept of Education As a Public Good 107

the provision, regulation and monitoring levels. This can be achieved as long as both public and private actors are democratic in their way of functioning and are responsible for building "alternative spaces in which critique is possible, practitioner knowledge can find expression and other trajectories for education are proposed" (Connell 2013: 285). In public and private schools alike, these phases should be grounded on democratic governance that implies transparent communication, and the participation of social and cultural actors existing in a particular context that have a say in the formulation of a negotiated educational project.

Placing the process of consultation at the centre of educational reform strategies implies a different view of the place occupied by education in the process of social consensus. Based on the recognition of other points of view and on the negotiation of common working methods, this process can represent "a mechanism through which these conflicts and tensions may be resolved by means of dialogue and agreed action" (Tedesco 1995: 108). This is an important condition, at least from a "formal", political perspective, when education is considered as a public good. Moreover, the governance of education can only be democratic if there is correspondence with the local characteristics, with regard to both the actors involved in the educational endeavour and to the content and ways in which education is implemented. This is why, following the classification by Higgins and Knight Abowitz (2011), "criteria of publicness" should also refer to "functional" factors, such as pedagogy and the curriculum.

5.3.2 Functional Conditions

Since both curriculum and pedagogy represent at the same time a technical and political issue, they should also be considered from a political point of view (Higgins and Knight Abowitz 2011). Thus, the ultimate responsibility for establishing curriculum standards and quality assurance mechanisms rests with the State. These conditions are essential for ensuring that quality education is made available for all. Appropriate investment in the training of teachers, the choice of relevant teaching methodologies and a diversified educational offer are essential components for the realization of a quality

108 R. Locatelli

education system. In the current context of educational governance, the participation of facilitating partners is therefore required:

> [C]ivic associations, community organizing groups, deliberative democracy organizations, and others must play a role in the public work described [...]. School administrators, school board members, and teachers have neither the time nor the training to handle this work alone, and it requires the energy and multiple perspectives that 'the people' can provide. [...] These resources represent an array of new knowledge, energy, and networks that school leaders of all kinds can tap into in order to help schools to be truly 'public'. (Knight Abowitz 2011: 488–489)

The political dimension of curriculum and pedagogy is inevitably connected with considerations of long-term and general interest in the choice of educational strategies. The greatest risk inherent in market mechanisms arises in particular from the inability of those involved to assume the long-term consequences of certain decisions due to their impossibility of "sacrificing immediate benefits" (Tedesco 1995). This implies reconnecting the content and methods of education to the broader purposes of schooling. Indeed, "[i]n preparing a democratic educational plan for the future, the first aspect that should be discussed is … the sense (or direction) of educational action" (Tedesco 1995: 72). The importance of the "qualification function" of education should not be disregarded, especially in light of the economic crisis and of increasing levels of unemployment, hence the greater attention to the quality of education. Indeed, an important function of schooling is inevitably connected with the fulfilment of private interests. However, an overemphasis on the "qualification" function may result in a somewhat restricted interpretation of the concept of *quality* education, understood almost exclusively in terms of easily measurable learning outcomes. As illustrated in the previous sections, this narrow focus on results, achieved through large-scale standardized testing, may result in narrowing the curriculum, teaching to the test and focusing instruction on aspects of learning that undermine what is needed for better local living, thus neglecting other important social dimensions of learning. Social, civic and political outcomes of educational processes can and must be assessed, even if they cannot necessarily

5 Reframing the Concept of Education As a Public Good

be measured (Tawil et al. 2012). In the design of curriculum and in the choice of methodologies, more emphasis should be placed on the so-called socialization and subjectification functions of education (Biesta 2009), related to "the goals associated with preparing students to actively and critically engage with the unprecedented diversity and complexity of contemporary social reality" (Keddie et al. 2011: 90). Pedagogies should promote critical thinking, social coexistence and reflect the local environment adopting methodologies that enhance multilingualism and multiculturalism.

Indeed, with respect to the growing trends of marketization of education, "critical pedagogy offers the capacity to use commercialism to criticize the broader structures of power informing its very presence in the school" (Saltman 2009: 39). This is how the abstract idea of "diversity" becomes a concrete matter of experience and the possibilities of mutual aid become shared learning and creative experiences. Education therefore becomes first and foremost a cultural matter rather than a commercial affair (Connell 2012). The participation of all actors, which reflects on the content and methods of teaching and learning can only be achieved in a democratic system, which puts greater emphasis on the public-good aspects of education.

5.3.3 Reframing the Theoretical Debate on Education in the Public Sphere

Although it has been argued that educational systems need to change significantly, a simple defence of the State is not useful to counterbalance the distortive effects of privatization in the field of education. It may also be necessary to accept that some kinds of private sector participation are more defensible than others and that some public sector "work" is not defensible at all (Burch 2009; Ball 2007). As argued earlier, the multifaceted process of privatization poses not only an economic challenge but also a political one, regarding the democratic functioning of institutions. In order to re-establish the *public* in the field of education, it is necessary to revisit those rules that have favoured the expansion of market ideologies at the expense of equality and democracy in both the private and public sectors. A recon-

110   R. Locatelli

stituted vision of the public and a set of practices and structures that support it should be grounded in the following principles:

> Trust and achievement can only emerge in a framework of public accountability that enables different accounts of public purpose and practice to be deliberated in a democratic public sphere: constituted to include difference, enable participation, voice and dissent, through to collective judgment and decision, that is in turn accountable to the public. (Apple 2006: 120)

The public sphere is certainly "under attack" as neo-liberal claims and managerial approaches have decreased the "space of criticism" (Apple 2006). However, the governance of education should not be considered as another education market since "[t]he market place excludes politics and leaves decision-making to the outcome of the rivalry between different groups representing individual, short-term interests" (Tedesco 1995: 108). Indeed, the difference between public policy, which should be a participatory and democratic process, and private markets in education is very important and ought to be safeguarded.

Education should undoubtedly be considered in the domain of the public. It has been argued that the public domain—or the public sphere (Habermas 1989 [1962])—denotes a particular quality of human interaction which is different from that of the private domain and of the market domain. The more normative perspective of the public sphere concerns the particular forms of action and relationship that are possible in "public" spaces (Biesta 2012). Building on the philosophy of Hannah Arendt, Gert Biesta acknowledges that the public is necessarily a space which makes political activity possible. The political and democratic understanding of freedom (different from liberal freedom-as-sovereignty) is seen as the defining quality for all action and is fundamentally interconnected with, and contingent upon, the freedom of others. The construction of public sphere is considered as an ongoing process of "becoming public" which is about

> the achievement of a form of human togetherness in which … action is possible and freedom can appear. (Biesta 2012: 693)

5 Reframing the Concept of Education As a Public Good   111

Within this perspective, education is seen as an essential component in the promotion of those forms of human action "through which freedom can appear". It is about rediscovering the political significance of education, which manifests itself as a concern for publicness, for the public quality of human togetherness. Strengthening public democratic institutions in order to favour the many, not the few (Reich 2015) is particularly important given the serious challenges that market arrangements in education pose to the principles of inclusion, equity and social justice in education. Indeed, reviving democratic involvement and public accountability may serve as a counter-balance to the influence of the market as well as to the limits of strong central and bureaucratic States "whose shortcomings have helped to legitimate the tendency to treat education as a private good rather than a public responsibility" (Whitty and Power 2000: 105).

At the same time, the State should promote democratic participation, allowing different stakeholders to have a say at all levels of the education endeavour. A State that is able and willing "to explore alternative transformative projects in which neoliberalism [...] is one subordinate element among others" (Jessop 2013: 73); one that is willing to invest in an educational proposal that is inevitably also a political project grounded on a cultural perspective where values of equity and equality of opportunity are not framed merely within economics but within a humanistic vision whereby education is seen as an opportunity for human beings to freely develop their full potential and to contribute to the democratic development and improvement of society (Dewey 1916).

The democratic process requires citizens capable of critique and contestation. In this light, democracy needs to be understood "as dynamic rather than static, as shot through with multiple power struggles, and as a quest and process, rather than an achieved state that must be fixed and held and protected" (Saltman 2009: 37). Based on the recognition of other points of view and on the negotiation of common working methods, this process can represent "a mechanism through which these conflicts and tensions may be resolved by means of dialogue and agreed action" (Tedesco 1995: 108).

The existence of a democratic system guaranteed by the State represents therefore the prerequisite for any action taken in view of the development of more inclusive and participatory institutions. However, changes in the way of functioning of institutions themselves need to be significant and "cannot be reduced to mere adjustments in a machine which has lost sight of its own purpose" (Tedesco 1995). A more inclusive way of functioning of public institutions requires a "shift in culture", combining top-down and bottom-up approaches (UNESCO 2016). As illustrated in previous sections, market-based approaches tend to provide easy responses to overcome the difficulties in education systems, by applying linear and standard solutions. Alternative models that are also practicable and sustainable are, on the contrary, considered as being much more complex and difficult to identify and to implement. As argued by Tedesco:

> Revolutionaries tend to be more lucid when putting forward diagnoses that justify change, but much less effective when it comes to presenting viable alternatives. (1995: 107)

The need to strengthen democratic institutions in a context of greater privatization and marketization requires more than a mere reaffirmation of the principle of education as a public good. It is fundamental to overcome the narrow economic framings of education by developing new approaches in order to integrate the notion of education as a public good with its fundamental social and cultural components which are often disregarded within standardized approaches. This is necessary to enhance transformative and alternative systems of governance that promote education not only as an economic tool for individual progress but, above all, as a collective endeavour for the fulfilment of human-beings and of their communities.

References

Apple, M. W. (2006). *Educating the "Right" Way: Markets, Standards, God and Inequality* (2nd ed.). New York: Routledge.

Ball, S. J. (2007). *Education Plc.* London: Routledge.

Ball, S. J. (2012). *Global Education Inc.* London: Routledge.

Bergan, S., Guarga, R., Egron Polak, F., Dias Sobrinho, J., Tandon, R., & Tilak, J. B. G. (2009). *Public Responsibility for Higher Education.* 2009 World Conference on Higher Education. Paris: UNESCO.

5 Reframing the Concept of Education As a Public Good 113

Biesta, G. J. J. (2009). Good Education in an Age of Measurement: On the Need to Reconnect with the Question of Purpose in Education. *Educational Assessment, Evaluation and Accountability, 21*(1), 33–46.

Biesta, G. J. J. (2012). Becoming Public: Public Pedagogy, Citizenship and the Public Sphere. *Social & Cultural Geography, 13*(7), 683–697.

Burch, P. (2009). *Hidden Markets. The New Education Privatization*. London: Routledge.

Caillods, F. (1997). The New Educational Environment: Planning by Participation. In F. Kemmer & D. Windham (Eds.), *Incentives Analysis and Individual Decision Making in the Planning of Education* (pp. 17–37). Paris: UNESCO/IIEP.

Connell, R. (2012). Just Education. *Journal of Education Policy, 27*(5), 681–683.

Connell, R. (2013). Why Do Market 'Reforms' Persistently Increase Inequality? *Discourse: Studies in the Cultural Politics of Education, 34*(2), 279–285.

Dewey, J. (1916). *Democracy and Education: An Introduction to the Philosophy of Education*. New York: Sheba Blake Publishing.

Education Commission. (2016). *The Learning Generation: Investing in Education for a Changing World*. The International Commission on Financing Global Education Opportunity.

Friedrich, D. (2016). Teach for All, Public-Private Partnerships, and the Erosion of the Public in Education. In A. Verger, C. Lubienski, & G. Steiner-Khamsi (Eds.), *The Global Education Industry. World Yearbook of Education 2016* (pp. 160–174). London: Routledge.

Habermas, J. (1989 [1962]). *The Structural Transformation of the Public Sphere* (T. Burger, Trans.). Cambridge, MA: MIT Press.

Heyneman, S. P., & Stern, J. M. (2014). Low Cost Private Schools for the Poor: What Public Policy Is Appropriate? *International Journal of Educational Development, 35*, 3–15.

Higgins, C., & Knight Abowitz, K. (2011). What Makes a Public School Public? *Educational Theory, 61*(4), 365–380.

Jessop, B. (2013). Putting Neoliberalism in Its Time and Place: A Response to the Debate. *Social Anthropology/Anthropologie Sociale, 21*(1), 65–74.

Keddie, A., Mills, M., & Pendergast, D. (2011). Fabricating an Identity in Neo-Liberal Times: Performing Schooling as "Number One". *Oxford Review of Education, 37*(1), 75–92.

Knight Abowitz, K. (2011). Achieving Public Schools. *Educational Theory, 61*(4), 467–489.

Levin, H. M. (2000). *The Public-Private Nexus in Education: Occasional Paper No. 1*. New York: National Center for the Study of Privatization in Education.

Levin, H. M. (2010). A Framework for Designing Governance in Choice and Portfolio Districts. In K. E. Bulkley, J. R. Henig, & H. M. Levin (Eds.), *Between Public and Private: Politics, Governance, and the New Portfolio Models for Urban School Reform* (pp. 217–250). Cambridge, MA: Harvard Education Press.

Lubienski, C. (2003). Instrumentalist Perspectives on the "Public" in Public Education: Incentives and Purposes. *Educational Policy, 17*(4), 478–502.

Macpherson, I., Robertson, S. L., & Walford, G. (Eds.). (2014). *Education, Privatization and Social Justice: Case Studies from Africa, South Asia and South East Asia.* Oxford: Symposium Books.

Minow, M. (2003). Public and Private Partnerships: Accounting for the New Religion. *Harvard Law Review, 116*(5), 1229–1270.

Ostry, J. D., Loungani, P., & Furceri, D. (2016). Neoliberalism: Oversold? *Finance & Development.* International Monetary Fund. Retrieved from www.imf.org/external/pubs/ft/fandd/2016/06/ostry.htm.

Ranson, S. (2008). Re-Constituting Education Governance for Cosmopolitan Society. In B. Lingard, J. Nixon, & S. Ranson (Eds.), *Transforming Learning in Schools and Communities the Remaking of Education for a Cosmopolitan Society* (pp. 184–206). London: Bloomsbury Publishing Plc.

Reich, R. (2015). *Saving Capitalism: For the Many, Not the Few.* New York: Alfred Knopf.

Rizvi, F. (2016). *Privatization in Education: Trends and Consequences.* ERF Working Papers Series, 18. Paris: UNESCO.

Saltman, K. J. (2009). Putting the Public Back in Public Schooling: Public Schools Beyond the Corporate Model. *DePaul Journal for Social Justice, 3*(1), 9–39.

Tawil, S., Akkari, A., & Macedo, B. (2012). *Beyond the Conceptual Maze: The Notion of Quality in Education.* ERF Occasional Papers, 2. Paris: UNESCO Education Research and Foresight.

Tedesco, J. C. (1995). *The New Educational Pact: Education, Competitiveness and Citizenship in Modern Society.* Geneva: IBE-UNESCO.

UNESCO. (2015). *Education 2030 Incheon Declaration and Framework for Action.* Paris: UNESCO.

UNESCO. (2016). *Education for People and Planet: Creating Sustainable Futures for All.* Global Education Monitoring Report 2016. Paris: UNESCO.

Verger, A., Lubienski, C., & Steiner-Khamsi, G. (2016). The Emergence and Structuring of the Global Education Industry: Towards an Analytical Framework. In A. Verger, C. Lubienski, & G. Steiner-Khamsi (Eds.), *The*

5 Reframing the Concept of Education As a Public Good

Global Education Industry. World Yearbook of Education 2016 (pp. 3–24). London: Routledge.

Walford, G. (2001). Privatization in Industrialised Countries. In H. M. Levin (Ed.), *Privatizing Education: Can the Marketplace Deliver Choice, Efficiency, Equity, and Social Cohesion?* (pp. 178–200). Boulder and Oxford: Westview Press.

Wettenhall, R. (2003). The Rhetoric and Reality of Public-Private Partnerships. *Public Organization Review: A Global Journal, 3,* 77–107.

Whitty, G., & Power, S. (2000). Marketization and Privatization in Mass Education Systems. *International Journal of Educational Development, 20,* 93–107.

6

Education As a Common Good

The revisited concept of education as a public good represents an essential principle for the democratic governance of education in a context characterized by greater privatization and marketization of education. The State should strengthen its responsibilities as the ultimate guarantor of the framework in which education policies and practices are developed, maintaining a fundamental role at all levels of the education endeavour, especially with regard to its regulatory function. These represent the essential conditions for the development of a democratic system wherein participation is possible and the right to education can be protected, respected and fulfilled. At the same time, it has been argued that it is necessary to reconsider the political element in education as a public good, which has been mostly framed in economic terms (Robertson 2018). Reframing education in the domain of the public entails strengthening public democratic institutions in order to favour the many, not the few (Reich 2015). The institutional and hierarchical relations typical of the "public" should deal with the need for greater participation in common decisions, with "the relationships that exist among the members of a society tied together in a collective endeavour" being emphasized (UNESCO 2015a: 78).

© The Author(s) 2019
R. Locatelli, *Reframing Education as a Public and Common Good,*
https://doi.org/10.1007/978-3-030-24801-7_6

In this perspective, the concept of common goods may represent a useful framework for the development of innovative approaches to educational governance in a democratic system. Indeed, the concept of common goods is increasingly adopted in philosophical-political spheres since its theoretical foundations are grounded in the alternative practices which oppose the spread of market policies that have been occurring both in the private and in the public domain. The multiplication of legal categories may be seen as a cause of concern for those who would support the need to keep referring to the consolidated categories of the *public* and *private*, which are presumed to be capable of giving answers to the governance of all kinds of goods. The reality of the nation-state should not be abandoned, but at the same time, it is necessary to consider the possibility of creating public institutions able to renew themselves and deal with change. Opening new avenues in the field of legal regulation means essentially facilitating a necessary cultural, ethical and political change (Viola 2016).

6.1 The Origins of the Concepts of Commons and of Common Goods

First and foremost, it is necessary to retrace the origins of the concept of the *commons* and of *common goods*. From the economic definition provided within neoclassical economic theory, according to which common-pool resources, or common goods, are characterized by the properties of rivalry and non-excludability, this concept has been applied to a variety of fields over the last few decades. In philosophical and political spheres, the concept of the *commons* has progressively replaced that of common-pool resources and has been applied to the governance of natural material resources (such as forests, fisheries, irrigation systems), as well as immaterial resources (such as knowledge and the Internet). Having said this, a more profound analysis of these concepts is essential in order to establish which of these categories may be more appropriately applied to the field of education.

6.1.1 Historical Background

The issue of commons and of common goods should not be confused with that of *the* common good. The latter, which dates back to Aristotle and inspired more or less all of Western philosophy, concerns the purposes and objectives for which a political society is constituted and differentiates from mere *de facto* coexistence. It denotes what is good in political and ethical terms. Therefore, *the* common good is not susceptible to ownership but instead it represents a norm or rule which unifies a political community.

The use of *"common"* as an adjective dates back to Roman law which designated a certain number of things as common (*res communes*), for example air, running water, the sea and its shores. These resources are considered as common by nature: that is, they cannot be owned and are for use by all. The concept of "common property" goes back to the thesis of Plato on the community property outlined in his dialogue the *Republic*. This line of thought influenced the work of Cicero and of Latin philosophical theories, as well as the natural law theories of Rousseau and Kant and the Utopian socialism of the mid-nineteenth century. However, it was not until the second half of the twentieth century that the issue of common goods, classified in standard economics also as common-pool resources or common property resources, became generally considered among scholars. The more recent interest in the issue around the *commons* is the result of several social and ecological threats which have been increasing since the late 1960s and which include destruction of resources and sites caused by population growth and industrial development. These issues were dealt with by Garrett Hardin, an American ecologist and philosopher, in 1968 in an article entitled *The Tragedy of the Commons* which appeared in the American journal *Science*. The author discussed the challenges of overpopulation in relation to the scarcity of resources of the planet. According to Hardin, the "tragedy of the commons" denotes a situation where an individual, acting independently and rationally according to its own self-interest, behaves against the best interests of the whole community by depleting some common resources.

In *The Tragedy of the Commons*, Hardin provides the example of a pasture shared in common by self-interested herders and demonstrates how this common resource would head towards inevitable ruin and degradation because of the individual actions of the herders (Locher 2013). The tragedy is expressed in Hardin's (1968: 1244) significant lines:

> Ruin is the destination toward which all men rush, each pursuing his own best interest in a society that believes in the freedom of the commons. Freedom in a commons brings ruin to all.

According to Hardin, it is only possible to avoid this tragedy in one of two ways: private ownership or direct administration imposed from outside, typically the State (Hardin 1968). "The tragedy of the commons", which denoted a quite intuitive and simple solution, became the starting point of any debate on the *commons*, a true intellectual challenge (Coccoli 2013). Indeed, "Hardin's either-or solution played a not insignificant part in the success of his argument, which [has been] put forward by enthusiasts both for the free market and for state intervention" (Locher 2016: 306).

However, there are some factors that make his simple message more complex and doubtful. In particular, it was argued that the choice of the term *commons* was used inappropriately and confusedly since common ownership did not directly apply to the case formulated by Hardin, whose analysis more generally referred to a situation of "lack of governance" (Locher 2016). In order to describe the behaviour of farmers, Hardin drew on a theory according to which society is reduced to the interaction of rival calculating individuals. The tragedy of the commons was framed within a "*rational choice paradigm*", "a general approach to human action based on an individualistic social cosmology" (Locher 2016: 308). This discourse produced a radical pessimism about the capacity of human groups to act collectively because of "free riding"[1] (Locher 2013).

During the 1970s, the "Tragedy" was countered by discourses that argued in favour of the legitimacy and effectiveness of community governance of resources and environments. For the purposes of this analysis, it is sufficient to recall briefly what Locher (2016) extensively illustrates

---

[1] Economic theory according to which individuals act independently for their own sake and personal return

6 Education As a Common Good   121

in his article regarding the historical roots of the commons paradigm.[2] Throughout the 1970s and 1980s, international studies aimed at demonstrating the appropriateness and sustainability of the *commons* paradigm. American anthropologists made a major contribution to showing that the *commons* could represent suitable and effective frameworks for governance in specific environmental, demographic and agricultural contexts. The possibility of developing local forms of cooperation inspired by indigenous institutions and other socio-cultural practices that favour effective and sustainable governance were subject to intense discussion at the World Bank, at the United Nations Educational, Scientific and Cultural Organization (UNESCO) and the Food and Agriculture Organization (FAO). As argued by Locher, the commons paradigm

> emerged from the crisis of the State and modernism as pillars of development. In the free-market-dominated 1980s, it offered another way forward. Drawing on the experience of the 1970s, it proposed making communities the main players in their own development. Poles apart from the modernist project, it identified in the accumulated wealth of social structures, vernacular practices and indigenous expertise the resources that could be mobilized, strengthened and restored. (2016: 327)

It is in line with these studies that in 1990 Elinor Ostrom formulated an innovative hypothesis on how to avoid the "tragedy of the commons". In her book *Governing the commons*, she demonstrated the baselessness of some of the implicit assumptions of the model developed by Hardin, based on her investigations on how communities succeeded or failed at managing the *commons*. Her critiques to Hardin's model are summarized as follows:

> Hardin's vivid narrative contains a number of contentions that commons scholars have repeatedly found to be mistaken: (1) he was actually discussing open access rather than managed commons; (2) he assumed little or no communication; (3) he postulated that people act only in their immediate self-interest (rather than assuming that some individuals take joint benefits

---

[2] The reviving of the discourse around commons started after the crisis in the Sahel region. For a detailed and exhaustive analysis on the roots of the commons paradigm see: Locher, F. (2016). Third World Pastures: The Historical Roots of the Commons Paradigm (1965–1990), *Quaderni Storici*, 2016 (1), 303–333.

into account, at least to some extent); (4) he offered only two solutions to correct the tragedy—privatization or government intervention. (Hess and Ostrom 2007: 11)

Ostrom asserted that human beings do not always respond to egoistic and self-interest logics and that there may exist some forms of cooperation that could serve as societal regulation in order to avoid the overconsumption of a specific good or resource. At the same time, these forms of cooperation would also make it possible to enlarge the community of beneficiaries (Ostrom 1990). She acknowledged how conditions of sustainability may be determined by communities themselves managing the resources that they share. In this respect, Ostrom rejects the overly schematic opposition between the State and the market, sustaining the existence of forms of governance and ownership that are different from public and private. In this perspective, unlike the notions of *public* and *private*, the *common* does not necessarily designate a system of ownership and belonging but rather a method of governance and of consumption (Nivarra 2012).

Although the classification of the *commons* has expanded to include natural, ecological, social and cultural goods, and more generically material and immaterial goods, it has been argued that this concept holds a minimum semantic core that can be traced as common in all sociopolitical claims, and which can be identified in the following features: (1) the opposition of the concept of *commons* to the dynamics of neoliberalism; (2) the re-composition of networks of cooperation within communities; (3) the development of instruments of participatory democracy (Coccoli 2013).

6.1.2 Different Applications of the Terms Commons and Common Goods

Before introducing the discussion on education, it is necessary to underline at this point a slight but important distinction between the use of the concept of the *commons* and of *common goods*. As aforementioned, the English term *commons* has progressively been used to refer to an institutional political space and has been largely applied to the governance of natural or immaterial resources, such as the environment or knowledge[3] where common governance may become a reality. Having said this, the term *commons* seems hardly applicable to goods or services such as education (or health) which necessarily require public institutions to play a predominant role in their regulation, monitoring, funding and provision.

Indeed, some scholars have dealt more closely with the concept of *common goods* from a philosophical political perspective and considered it as a stand-alone category which goes beyond the economic classification of goods (Taylor 1995; Deneulin and Townsend 2007; Viola 2016). In this way, shared governance is not justified on the basis of an economic rationale but more importantly on the basis of the cultural and social value of a specific good (Deneulin and Townsend 2007; Taylor 1995). In fact, Hess and Ostrom (2007) acknowledge that the term commons "is not value laden" (p. 14). Education, on the contrary, does raise issues about values, politics and the social nature of our thinking.

The broadened conceptualization of the term common goods seems more appropriate for the governance of services, or goods, that need to be provided and managed concretely. However, the way this concept is defined and used in this analysis should not be confused with the concept as it is framed within the economic theory that presupposes rational-optimizing actors. When dealing with "common goods", it should be noted that it is not about "goods" as defined in the economic theory of public–private goods but rather "goods" understood in the broadest possible sense, as a whole set of tools, activities, values, rights and processes that would benefit everyone. As such, the concept of common goods refers to a recently developed legal and political framework which, although not as radically as the concept of the *commons*, does add something relevant to the discussion on the governance of education conducted so far in terms of vision, popular participation and democratic processes. It is this socio-philosophical interpretation of common goods which is considered in this analysis. The use of the concept of common

---

[3] See, for instance: Hess, C. and Ostrom, E. (2007). *Understanding Knowledge as a Commons: From Theory to Practice.* The MIT Press. https://mitpress.mit.edu/books/understanding-knowledge-commons

goods is preferable to that of commons as the latter seems hardly applicable to goods or services such as education which necessarily require public institutions to play an important role in their governance.

According to this interpretation, *common goods* have been defined as those goods that exist only when there are common actions in their production and in their consumption. The benefits and burdens for the realization of these goods are intrinsically *shared* among all participants—not opposed (as for *private* goods), or "notwithstanding" (as for *public* goods) (Viola 2016). Indeed, "common" means *com-muniis*, that is, the equal sharing of duties and responsibilities, and is contrary to "immune", *in-muniis*, without duties. Goods of this kind are grounded in a strong sense of the relationships that exist within a community, and are identified as the typical model of political cooperation. For instance, Charles Taylor has distinguished between "decomposable" and "convergent" goods as opposed to "common" goods. The author asserts that public goods are essentially conceived as "decomposable" goods in the ordinary understanding within welfarism (Taylor 1995). Public goods are considered individual goods, since they "cannot be procured for one person without being secured for a whole group. But the goods it produces are surely those of individuals" (p. 55). In this perspective, the production and consumption process of public goods is directly characterized by an individualistic and utilitarian approach which conceives the specific goods as decomposable and instrumentally valuable. Moreover, there may also be public goods which are "convergent", produced by a cooperative action but then enjoyed individually. On the contrary, within common goods, the shared action is intrinsic, as well as instrumental, both to the goods itself and to its benefits acquired in the course of that shared action. Goods of this kind are therefore inherently common in their "production" and in their benefits (Deneulin and Townsend 2007). Although there are ways in which common goods have a non-excludable and non-rivalrous character like public goods, it is argued that "these two features are presented in terms of participation and generation of the goods themselves and not in terms of consumption of a commodity" (Deneulin and Townsend 2007: 18). The *common* quality of these goods is not pre-existing but is dynamic and contingent. Common goods contribute to, and are the result of, the interaction among the different components of

6 Education As a Common Good 125

society and, since they are essential to a life in common, they cannot be reduced to economic resources or to factors of production (Donolo 2012).

Common goods should inevitably be considered as *relational* goods, because they can be achieved and can be enjoyed only with others (Viola 2016; Arena and Iaione 2012; Donati and Solci 2011). Moreover, common goods determine the ways in which the relations of people with goods define and model fundamental rights themselves. The nature of common goods not only contributes to the identification of some fundamental rights but also requires a necessary link between common fruition and common governance. This gives personal rights not only an individualistic and subjective meaning but implies a relational conception of human rights, in terms of their entitlement and pursuit, both regarding the relationships between persons and the relationship between persons and goods, which necessarily depend on the existence of certain goods and on their specific configuration (Viola 2016).

Moreover, it has been argued that this category has also a functionalist nature, in that resources become "common goods" once they appear fundamental to the realization of a particular social goal that is coherent with political-democratic instances of a certain community (De Toffol and Valastro 2012). The processes of privatization of the last decades and the progressive dismantling of the welfare state have increased the interest in this category of goods and in their defence. Their nature makes it necessary to overcome the logics of property. The choice of public or private becomes irrelevant because it is exclusive, whereas a logic of *accessibility* and *inclusion* that characterizes common goods is preferable. Hence, the need to ensure methods of participated management of these resources that, when not expressed as forms of common ownership, have at least to be expressed in forms of governance and be protected on behalf of the community through forms of participation that acknowledge the right of people to act in order to safeguard, protect and guarantee these goods (De Toffol and Valastro 2012).

On the basis of this analysis, Table 6.1 aims to represent a systematic and detailed framework with the different dimensions that should be considered when comparing the concepts of public goods and of common goods. It highlights the foundational principles and theories on which the two concepts are grounded, the different nature of public and

126   R. Locatelli

Table 6.1 Public goods versus common goods

	Public goods	Common goods
Principles/ theories	Equity and social justice	Besides equity and social justice, also solidarity and cooperation
	Political economy theory	Philosophical and political perspective
	Subjective conception of rights	Relational conception of rights
Nature	Can be enjoyed as individual goods	Necessarily shared, both regarding production and benefits
	Non-excludable and non-rivalrous characteristics presented in terms of consumption of a commodity	Non-excludable and non-rivalrous characteristics presented in terms of participation and generation of the goods themselves
	The public quality is predetermined	The common quality is dynamic and not pre-existing
Governance	Public governance justified on the basis of externalities which extend to all	Shared governance justified on the basis of the cultural and social value of a specific good
	Result of the action of public institutions	Result of the interaction of the different components of society
	Top-down approach	Bottom-up approach
	Passive role of those who benefit	Active role of those who benefit
	Formal democracy	Substantial participatory democracy
Value	Limited to the provision of facilities and services to a certain national community	Necessarily imply the empowerment of all actors who have a right to a fully informed and critical participation
	Neutral context	Acknowledgment of the diversity of contexts and of the cultural and social dimensions of a specific community
	Instrumental, can be treated as economic resources	Cannot be reduced to economic resources or to factors of production because of intrinsic social and relational value

6 Education As a Common Good   127

common goods and the characteristics of these two. These different qualities have implications and promote different forms of governance and political regimes. Finally, differences can also be found in the values underpinning these two concepts.

6.2 The Concept of Education As a Common Good[4]

The problem of giving legal form to the category of common goods largely depends on the dominant paradigm which considers as "natural" the power of the State or of the market with regard to different domains of social life. However, if we tried leaving this cultural preconditioning aside for a moment, common goods would lose their characteristic of exception and, the power of the State, or of the market, would need adequate justification. This is also the case with education which, when considered as a natural process, should take place irrespectively of any institutionalized intervention.[5] Without taking into account any degree of institutional absence and bearing in mind the characteristics and challenges of current realities and institutions, the concept of common goods may represent an interesting perspective to adopt when looking at different aspects of the "good" education, even with regard to basic and compulsory levels. This is all the more fundamental especially when considering the crisis of welfare states in many countries worldwide, the blurring of boundaries between the public and the private, and the emergence of mixed, hybrid forms promoting conceptions of education as a marketable, private good.

As well as reaffirming the importance of the principle of education as a public good, considering education as a common good may provide the elements on which to build alternative and more inclusive approaches to schooling in order to counter merely economic and utilitarian solutions

---

[4] This perspective builds on the foundational publication realized by UNESCO: UNESCO. (2015). *Rethinking Education: Towards a global common good?* Paris: UNESCO

[5] See in this respect, the work of Ivan Illich (*Deschooling Society*, 1973), Paul Goodman (*Compulsory Miseducation*, 1971) or Paulo Freire (*Pedagogy of the Oppressed*, 1970).

which may contribute to the spreading of inequalities worldwide. It is about responding to the failures of governments to deliver quality education not by relying on market-based approaches to schooling, or returning to the ways of functioning of highly centralized bureaucratic states, but by envisaging new and innovative public institutions that can improve quality and efficiency thanks to the empowerment of and the greater cooperation among the forces present in society. This may be practicable in contexts with different characteristics but requires minimum democratic conditions since it builds on the free and responsible participation of the diverse forces existing in society. These conditions may be present in different degrees and may have different forms, but the objective and the method of work remain similar.

If compared to the current ways of functioning of the welfare systems, however, the principle of education as a common good does not propose easy paths. It calls for a revisiting of existing societal equilibriums in order to reactivate capacities to innovate and rethink welfare systems substantially. It introduces challenging elements with regard to highly consolidated operational habits. Indeed, communality may result in the most profound conflict the composition of which remains temporary. A society, however, may be able to cope with confrontation and conflict and therefore be enriched by the pluralism of positions, as long as it is able to practise cooperation in common decisions, while preserving what cannot be negotiated (Viola 2012). For these reasons, the possibility of considering education as a common good depends on a strong political commitment, willing to call into question current cultural orientations and institutions in order to promote innovation and social change based on the values of human dignity and freedom.

6.2.1 Reaffirming a Humanistic Vision of Education, Beyond Utilitarianism and Individualism

Overcoming the utilitarian tradition of "decomposable goods" (Taylor 1995), the notion of common goods suggests that education incorporates common understandings of its value, grounded in specific cultural and social backgrounds. From a "common good" perspective, "it is not only the 'good life' of individuals which matters but also the goodness of the life that humans hold in common" (Deneulin and Townsend 2007: 9). Indeed, common goods are identified for their contribution to the "general interest" to conditions of justice and well-being. In this perspective, the concept of common goods at the micro-level is related to the idea of *the* common good at the macro-level, "understood in terms of social solidarity, social relations based on universal human rights and equality of respect" (Marginson 2016: 16).

As mentioned earlier, common goods are relational goods since they can be realized only within a relational process. This vision highlights the collective dimension and the purposes of education as a common societal endeavour, based on the acknowledgement that relationships are the foundation of each process of "production" or "fruition" of common goods. Stressing the importance of relationships is all the more necessary with regard to current socio-economic realities, where the representation of the *homo economicus* has prevailed over a vision that conceives the human being inserted in a community/society (Franzini 2012). This cultural orientation, also reflected in neo-classical economics, is at the origin of individual behaviour which is oriented towards individual success or enrichment. In this respect, the theory of common goods aims to promote an alternative vision of human well-being, underlining people's altruistic and cooperative attitudes. The recent economic and financial crisis has highlighted the limits of the economic approach that has characterized the last decades and has allowed for the exploration of different visions on which to found economic and social dynamics.

Education as a common good calls into question the current utilitarian model which conceives education as a mere individual socio-economic investment. It favours a humanistic approach which places the person and his/her connections with the community at the centre. It implies the enhancement of the cultural, social and relational dimensions of each educational process. Inspired by a sense of dignity and solidarity among human beings, the participatory process should promote the expression of the diversity of contexts, worldviews and knowledge systems. At different levels of the education system, it would imply that different forms of education, be they formal or non-formal, could nurture each other in a reciprocal process, giving voice and representation to the different groups present in society. It is about the opportunity of making education more relevant to the specificities of different realities in a creative and inclusive process of empowerment. In this perspective, education is the result of a process of co-production between the public and all the other components of society. Even before it is taken by institutions, which tend to retain the existing state, this opportunity should be seized by society. The task is to introduce and extend practices of innovation able to generate new scenarios and new forms of social cooperation and coexistence. Education as a common good could become an effective democratic exercise through which the actors negotiate and restructure the institutional framework in which they are involved (Nicolas-Le Strat 2015).

6.2.2 Community Participation

As aforementioned, overcoming the classical dichotomy between the public and the private, common goods are defined by their management arrangements and by their methods of shared governance. At the different levels of the educational process, the participatory process should be based on the sharing of values and objectives, aiming to promote processes of co-participation and integration of responsibilities and resources, both human and economic, as well as of risks and benefits. In this perspective, the nature of the actors does not change; they remain "public" and "private". What changes is the object and the method of work. Private actors would not result as mere service lenders, students and families would no longer be considered as "consumers" or merely "users" but would be qualified as active components in the processes of policy development and implementation. The underlying perspective is grounded on the belief that everyone is entitled to contribute and have a say regarding education seen as a common good—students, families, teachers, educators, civil society, researchers or the private sector. Indeed, the quest for *the* common good, which is the aim of any democratic society, is considered not only a prerequisite of institutional public authorities but begins within society itself (Viola 2016).

At the same time, the process of participation which characterizes the approach to education as a common good "is a common good in itself. The shared action is intrinsic, as well as instrumental, to the good itself,

6 Education As a Common Good 131

with benefits derived also in the course of shared action" (UNESCO 2015a: 78). This concept necessarily promotes a greater consideration of the importance of the local contexts and of the different forces that are already present within a given society which are directly involved in the governance of education at different levels.

As illustrated above, this participation and co-construction cannot obviously replace the welfare system guaranteed by the State. It can, however, integrate it, concur with it both practically and ideally, with the circulation and sharing of resources that would otherwise be totally privatized, or unused (Brunod et al. 2016). Considering education as a common good implies that all actors with a stake in education take part in the process of production of education services. Indeed, education takes place not only in schools but also within families, communities and societies. For instance, in analysing the "production" process of public education, Porter (2012) observes that students and families bring an essential contribution. Co-production implies that students are not merely users but acquire an active role in "co-producing" education. Indeed, inputs from the students are essential for the creating of education opportunities of good quality since there can be no learning without their active, willing participation. Moreover, significant inputs are provided from outside the classroom by parents, peers, community organizations and others. If these inputs are few or omitted, education services may still be created but will have very different qualities and quantities. A democratically functioning system would therefore create the opportunities which encourage a more varied family and community participation in order to improve the quality of public institutions (Porter 2012).

More in general, the participation of community to the educational process may contribute to the identification of local education issues and to develop strategies to resolve barriers that impede access and retention and compromise quality. Civic participation in the life of local schools also helps to ensure the relevance of the curriculum and its delivery. It can also be an effective component in monitoring the process and outcomes of education at multiple levels. In resource-constrained settings, community participation can also serve as an effective means for mobilizing and maximizing the resources needed to move towards a high-quality system of education (Uemura 1999). Community participation in education is

132   R. Locatelli

seen as a way to improve monitoring and accountability of schools to the community they serve. For instance, "in places where teacher absenteeism and poor performance are critical issues, parents can be part of the system of monitoring and supervising teachers, ensuring that teachers arrive at classrooms on time and perform effectively in the classrooms" (Uemura 1999: 4). As a result, community participation may contribute to the improvement of equitable access, quality and performance of schooling. Indeed,

> [l]ocal community participation in assessing needs by means of a dialogue with the public authorities and groups concerned in society is a first, essential stage in broadening access to education and improving its quality [...]. When communities assume greater responsibility for their own development, they learn to appreciate the role of education both as a way of achieving societal objectives and as a desirable improvement of the quality of life. (Delors et al. 1996: 29)

There are plenty of institutional arrangements which are formed by communities themselves and which often prove more effective than the typical "all-public" and "all-private" solutions in safeguarding shared resources. Examples of this can be found in the recent report by Rossignoli and Riggall (2019) *Innovation and achievement: the work of four not-for-profit school groups* which illustrates how such organizations have succeeded in expanding access to quality education to hard-to-reach groups thanks to greater social commitment, autonomy, accountability, flexibility in the use of limited resources and investment in teacher training. It should be noted that experiences which draw in the direction of a greater account of the diversity of contexts and stronger participation of communities can be found at different levels of education, ranging from compulsory schooling to alternatives in higher education which fall outside of the mainstream university model (McCowan 2016).

The need to strengthen the role of communities and to form "new and revitalized partnerships" corresponded to the "expanded vision" held by signatories to the World Declaration on Education for All in 1990, later echoed in the *Delhi Declaration* (UNESCO 1994). The need to declare the importance of partnerships resulted from the acknowledgement that the role of the State in education systems was changing and its central

6 Education As a Common Good 133

function seriously being questioned. Indeed, "[F]or governments in low-income countries, the possibility of greater contributions to education by the private sector held out the prospect of increased sharing of the heavy load of operating education systems" (Bray 1999: 8). The *Delhi Declaration* (clause 2.8) included the statement that

> education is, and must be, a societal responsibility, encompassing governments, families, communities and non-governmental organizations alike; it requires the commitment and participation of all, in a grand alliance that transcends diverse opinions and political positions.

Community partnerships may provide an appropriate balance between an excessively bureaucratic and inflexible government and the risk of inequalities and fragmentation deriving from State absence and greater participation of private (for-profit) actors. The precise nature of this balance of course varies in different situations and "historical legacies" should be taken into consideration (Bray 1999). It has also come to light that whenever community participation has been mandated from the top, problems related to modalities of implementation have surfaced (Oxfam India 2014). As also acknowledged by Apple and Beane (1995) in their book *Democratic Schools*, successful partnerships require "the conscious building of coalitions within the school and between the school and constituencies outside it. In none of the cases was the impetus generated from the 'top.' Instead, bottom-up movements—groups of teachers, the community, social activists, and so on—provided the driving force for change" (pp. 13–14).

Together with the greater participation of communities, civil society organizations and other non-state actors also play a crucial role in the advancement of education systems in ways that are culturally and socially sensitive. The role of civil society organizations as partners of governments in the production and governance of education deserves specific attention. Indeed, they received particular prominence both at the Jomtien World Conference in 1990 and at Incheon in 2015. Their role has developed considerably in the last two decades and many partnerships between governments and non-governmental organizations (NGOs) achieve results which would otherwise have been impossible. As envisaged in the Framework for Action for Education 2030, civil society organizations:

134   R. Locatelli

promote social mobilization and raise public awareness, enabling the voices of citizens (particularly those who face discrimination) to be heard in policy development;

develop innovative and complementary approaches that help advance the right to education, especially for the most excluded groups;

document and share evidence from practice, from citizens' assessments and from research to inform structured policy dialogue, holding governments accountable for delivery, tracking progress, undertaking evidence-based advocacy, scrutinizing spending and ensuring transparency in education governance and budgeting. (UNESCO 2015b: 80)

In addition to civil society organizations, which fulfil a distinctive role in the protection of communities, the private sector is also considered as playing a fundamental role in education (Education Commission, UNESCO, World Bank). The adoption of an approach to education seen as a common good, however, implies that a paradigm change occurs also in the way in which economic actors and relations are conceived. It is argued that purely economic actors should recall the very origins of economic doctrines, which centre around relationships between people, rediscovering ethical principles and virtues that may guide innovative approaches to a "humanistic economy", instead of being purely economic transaction (Bruni 2012). Indeed, although market mechanisms may seem more effective and efficient in increasing educational opportunities and funding, their solutions remain highly standardized and not necessarily linked to the local contexts, often leading to forms of exclusion and discrimination. Instead of promoting competition as a tool for greater efficiency and effectiveness, economic actors should also encourage forms of cooperation. Indeed, it is widely acknowledged in several domains, from natural to social sciences, that cooperation is often more convenient than competition. The aim here is not to condemn or totally dismiss all forms of competition but rather to ascribe them to a broader framework of cooperation grounded on values of solidarity, equity, social justice, shared responsibility and mutual accountability. In this respect, direct or indirect forms of privatization, leading to the exclusion or externalization of functions based on mere economic competition or efficiency logics, or for the sake of profit, would hardly result compatible with the conception of education as a common good.

6 Education As a Common Good   135

Of course, "the call for people's mobilization must not be a justification for the state to abdicate its responsibilities" (UNDP 1997: 101). The State should maintain a key role in protecting the interests of the poor and this is certainly one of the implications when considering education primarily as a *public* good. At the same time, it should renew itself by strengthening its essential functions and responsibilities of regulation, control and promotion of innovation in education (Arena and Iaione 2012). It remains institutionally responsible for the planning, designing and realization of the educational system, operating both in a "vertical" position (as primary responsible) and in a "horizontal" position (as one of the actors involved in the process). These forms of cooperation, based on mutual trust, reliability and willingness to change, would allow the realization of the best combination of efficiency, inclusiveness and equity in the governance of education. To achieve this, it is necessary for the organizational functioning to be transparent, and for assessment and punctual reporting to be implemented. The ultimate responsibility remains in the hands of the State which is accountable for the spending and for the use of public resources. Indeed, the concept of common goods suggests that the actors involved promote forms of cooperation aimed at integrating or transforming the public rather than undermining it.

6.2.3   Towards Participatory Democracy

It is argued that the highest form of direct community and citizen participation undoubtedly takes place at the level of decision-making: problem identification, feasibility-study, planning, implementation and evaluation (Shaeffer 1994; Reimers 1997). In this light, a change is also needed in the way in which public and governmental power is exerted. In a welfare society, the function of the government goes beyond the hierarchical logics and characterizes itself by openness, participation and responsibility of the governance. It is an enlarged function of governance which aims to coordinate and integrate a plurality of actors, values, rationalities and different cultures while respecting their specificities and autonomy. A form of governance which favours consensual and negotiated relationships, opposed to the traditional vertical and hierarchical one. Indeed,

136   R. Locatelli

"placing common goods beyond the public or private dichotomy implies conceiving and aspiring towards new forms and institutions of participatory democracy" (UNESCO 2015a: 78).

The concept of common goods encourages the review of "the old top-down, orderly, and hierarchical categories of social structure and social authority" (Cahill 2005: 45). It is about the adoption of new forms of direct participation based on the concept of subsidiarity, an organizational criterion of institutional bodies inspired by the principles of cooperation and solidarity. Indeed, subsidiarity normally has a twofold meaning: vertical and horizontal. In the first sense, it refers to multilevel government, that is, the allocation of responsibilities to minor local bodies, and progressively to the major regional, national institutional bodies on the basis of capacity, efficiency and effectiveness. In the second sense, it refers to forms of cooperation between the public and private, according to which the public facilitates the activities of the private for the general interest (De Toffol and Valastro 2012). Within such perspective, the public institution places itself as close as possible to the citizens, promoting their participation in common decisions. In this way, the principle of subsidiarity has to be reconceived and "its connotation of a vertical dynamic of influence is expanded to include horizontal and 'transversal' exercises of authority and efficacy, characterized by power sharing" (Cahill 2005). Based on a cooperative alliance between public and private actors, and on the sharing of resources in the general interest, the principle of subsidiarity would allow the improvement of community well-being with respect for the freedom and dignity of all people.

Democracy could become truly inclusive because it would not only be based on voting but would be guaranteed by the active participation of all components of society as well. This is necessary to move from *formal* democracy, which is mainly an "aggregative technique" and limits itself to representation, to *participatory* democracy, which is the most effective way for society to put forward its visions of well-being (Viola 2012). The involvement of communities, civil society and other non-state actors in the building and implementation of public policies represents one of the fundamental features of the discussion on institutional democratization and quality of decisional processes.

6 Education As a Common Good 137

This model of participatory democracy which is essential within an approach to education seen as a common good is based on cooperation and not on the delegation of power or the exclusive exercise thereof. Moreover, the objective of participation is not the claim for power in itself but rather the constant relationship between public, civic and private actors that should characterize the entire decision-making process (policy design, analysis and implementation). In institutional and political terms, participatory democracy needs to translate into organizational and procedural rules, in order to guarantee the fairness and effectiveness of participatory process and the fulfilling of the right of all actors to participate in political processes (De Toffol and Valastro 2012). Moreover, participation has to be necessarily collective if it is to influence policy processes. The essential connection between collective action and power was also acknowledged by Hannah Arendt in *The Human Condition* (1958) where she defined *power* as the capacity to act in common and to start new actions.

The concept of education as a common good encourages democratization of the decision-making process, both in the governance of structures and processes of schools, as well as in the design and formulation of curriculum and pedagogy, which should be made accessible to community groups. Committees, councils and other decision-making groups include not only professional educators but also young people, their parents and other members of the school community (Apple and Beane 1995). It is argued that this kind of democratic planning, at both the school and the classroom levels, does not represent "the 'engineering of consent' toward predetermined decisions that has too often created the illusion of democracy, but a genuine attempt to honor the right of people to participate in making decisions that affect their lives" (Apple and Beane 1995: 6). This set of commitments has been demonstrated to work in powerful ways. In Brazil, for instance, the Citizen School and "participatory budgeting" have provided exceptional models of how democratic education can change the lives of students, teachers and entire communities (Apple and Beane 2007). This set of policies and the accompanying processes of implementation are constitutive parts of a clear and explicit project aimed at constructing not only a better school for the excluded but also a larger project of radical democracy. A common-good approach to education enables the creation and development of educational transformations coming from the "periphery" and not from those who "arrogate the 'center' to themselves" (Gandin and Apple 2002: 26).

The existence of participatory institutions is also considered important for the improvement of accountability mechanisms within public institutions. Indeed, the call for parents and community members to take part in school governance is seen as a way to increase the accountability of public services. The UNESCO Global Education Monitoring Report team acknowledges that "strengthening participatory accountability is considered an effective strategy for building equitable education systems and providing quality education" (UNESCO 2016a). Participatory accountability emphasizes the importance of participation of parents and of the community in the education process. Schools are accountable to families not through the mechanisms of choice but through families having a voice and opportunities for dialogue on school governing bodies.

Those in favour of participation, however, also acknowledge that exercising democracy involves tensions and contradictions. Democratic participation in decision-making, for example, opens the way for anti-democratic ideas such as the continuing demands for censorship of materials, the use of public tax vouchers for private school tuition and the maintenance of historical inequities in school life. Furthermore, there is always the possibility of the illusion of democracy, in which authorities may invite participation so as to "engineer consent" for predetermined decisions (Graebner 1988). These elements point to the fact that creating democracy is always a struggle. The identification of solutions which are context-sensitive and which contribute to the democratization of the system are therefore far from simple. Indeed, "democracy is a dynamic concept that requires continuous examination in light of changing times" (Apple and Beane 1995: 13). Having said this, beyond these contradictions lies the possibility for all actors in society "to work together in creating more democratic schools that serve the common good of the whole community" (Apple and Beane 2007: 5). Empowering citizens and communities to make important decisions about the institutions in which they live and work is probably the most effective way to make educational opportunities and governance more sustainable and equitable.

6.2.4 An Integrated and Inter-sectorial Approach

Education as a common good promotes active citizenship, equality and community reinforcement and empowerment, which in turn represents preconditions for effective participation in the democratic process. Indeed, in order for processes in education to be truly participatory, it is essential that all actors become aware of their role as citizens and therefore assume responsibility for their actions. Responsibility is defined as the ability to become aware of certain values and to ensure a response adapted to a known, foreseen and possible risk (Meyer-Bisch et al. 2016).

The "social connection model" of responsibility developed by Marion Young (2005) is strictly connected with the recognition of education as a collective endeavour. According to Young, all moral agents, both individual and institutional, have the responsibility to eliminate injustices which arise from inequality and disparity. Of course, she emphasizes that those who are "institutionally and materially situated to be able to do more to affect the conditions of vulnerability have greater obligations" (p. 712). This is why the concept of education as a public good should remain a valid framework according to which the role of the State is ensured as the ultimate guarantor of the public sphere. At the same time, it is acknowledged that education is a collective and social responsibility which involves all actors, although at different levels.

However, in order for processes in education to become truly democratic, it is essential that all actors—from public institutions to the private sector, community organizations, households or individuals—are in the condition to assume responsibility. This requires that all actors "have a right to fully informed and critical participation in creating school policies and programs for themselves and young people" (Apple and Beane 2007: 5). The development of awareness and the assumption of responsibilities therefore require an integrated and inter-sectorial approach based on the principle of lifelong learning as reaffirmed in the Education 2030 agenda. Indeed, given the greater complexity and unprecedented changes in the education landscape, there is a need to re-contextualize the right to education, so that it is not limited to the right to schooling but is also extended to the right to lifelong learning

(McCowan 2013; Chakroun and Daelman 2018). Not only should children and young people have access to an education system of good quality but also adults throughout life should be able to acquire, or strengthen, their capabilities in order to act as aware and responsible citizens. Appropriate educational solutions should therefore be designed and made available for different groups in society. An integrated approach, "based on renewed ethical and moral foundations", should also take into consideration the diversity of cultures and systems of knowledge, and therefore consider the involvement and support of all communities and minorities, each with their different knowledge systems (UNESCO 2015a: 83). Integrating formal, non-formal and informal education is an essential element for the development of an inclusive educational project aiming at the strengthening of democracy.

Considering education as a common good therefore implies an integrated approach to education which may favour the transformation of public institutions in order to overcome more hierarchical and utilitarian approaches and build more democratic schooling systems. This requires that students, families, communities and other actors are prepared and acquire the capabilities to take part freely and responsibly in the educational process (Walker 2018). The concept of common goods highlights the collective and socio-cultural dimensions of education and aids the formulation of education policies and practices aimed at promoting freedom and strengthening capabilities. Indeed, the capability approach can be considered as an essential component within the framework of education seen as a common good. As argued by Robeyns,

> when asking normative questions, we should ask what people are able to do and what lives they are able to lead. The capability approach cares about people's real freedoms to do these things, and the level of wellbeing that they will reach when choosing from the options open to them. It is a rich, multidimensional approach. (Robeyns 2017: 7)

These conditions are essential for ensuring that people can take responsibility for effective participation in political and civic life and therefore contribute to the strengthening of democratic institutions which in turn could favour the development of more inclusive and equitable educational opportunities (Fig. 6.1).

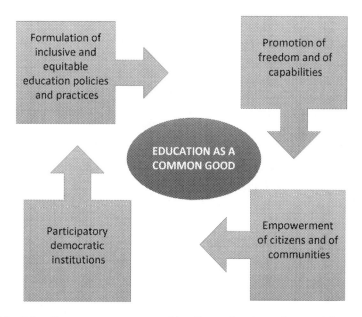

Fig. 6.1 Education as a common good implies an integrated approach

Giving the people the possibility to free and responsible participation is essential for the effective exercise of popular sovereignty, which should be the ultimate goal of a true democracy. Popular sovereignty not only comprises formal procedures of political participation but expresses itself also in a daily culture of democracy. In this regard, the sovereignty of the nation-state should be seen as conditioned by popular involvement, to be maintained, rebuilt and developed through innovative ways of participation that are culturally adapted (Meyer-Bisch et al. 2016).

The education sector on its own cannot be counted on to optimally identify responses and provide solutions to wide-ranging challenges. In this perspective, the concept of education as a common good calls for greater cooperation both within and beyond the education sector in order to substantially innovate and rethink education systems. A multi-stakeholder collaborative approach should involve government, civil society and the private sector, as well as other sectors such as health, social, financial and economic services. Indeed, education needs to work with other sectors to change daily and community behaviours (UNESCO

142   R. Locatelli

2016b). The free participation of all actors, especially of communities and families in educational governance can only truly take place when stability, safety and security measures have been fulfilled. Moreover, there should be increasing interactions between all sectors also to develop up-to-date education systems that take full advantage of technological innovations while maintaining equity and ethics in education.

6.3   Education, Beyond Public to Common Good: A Continuum

As previously illustrated, considering education as a public good implies that the State maintains and strengthens, above all, the responsibility for ensuring the regulatory framework within which education is provided, funded and monitored. In this perspective, the concept of education as a public good enhances the development of democratic processes where the participation of all actors in the formulation of policies and practices is foreseen in order to achieve a public-good approach to education which aims at achieving free and quality education for all. Within a public-good approach, the point of view remains essentially focused on public institutions that should provide the regulatory framework for the development of democratic educational systems.

In order to bring about a significant change in the way of functioning of public institutions, however, it is necessary that a "shift in culture" occurs that considers more profoundly the relevance of contexts and the neglected social and cultural dimensions of education in order to promote a greater complementation of both top-down and bottom-up approaches (UNESCO 2016b). In fact, the need to reconnect public institutions with "the people" has been widely manifested in many countries worldwide. Critiques towards the vertical and hierarchical, and often not transparent, ways of functioning of governments is the product of the delusions produced by a political approach and governance that leave the principle of "popular sovereignty" often unmet (Valastro 2010). It is precisely at this point that the concept of education as a common good comes into play with its significant political and cultural background which considers democracy and the principle of participation as inextricably linked. Considering education as a common good implies that education is a collective shared endeavour, both in its production and in its benefits. It implies that students themselves, and all actors in general, are considered as directly responsible for the development of the educational project of a given community. This is in line with the fulfilment of the right to education as framed in a relational approach, which should be seen as the responsibility of the community as a whole, not only of public institutions (Meyer-Bisch et al. 2016).

Of course, the democratic participation of all actors in the educational endeavour can be possible only in a framework of governance that is guaranteed by the State. That is why the concepts of education as a public and common good can be seen in a sort of continuum and do not exclude each other. Indeed, it should be emphasized that the principle of the common goods as applied to education does not diminish the importance of the role of the State in education. It rather implies a strengthening of its function of regulation while calling for a revisiting of the institution itself. In this respect, the importance of conceiving education as a public good should not be disregarded, especially in those contexts where educational systems have not been fully realized or developed.

As mentioned in previous chapters, goods exhibit the aspects of a private, public, and therefore of a common good, simultaneously. As a public good, the regulation, monitoring and assessment of the educational system remain primarily the responsibility of the State. At the same time, education is a social and cultural matter and it is the process through which human beings fully develop. The concept of the common is greater than the notion of the private and public. It encompasses them in an attempt to introduce a different perspective on how education systems should be organized and for what purposes. It is the adoption of a necessary cultural change.

This research suggests a revisited formulation of the classification by Katarina Tomaševski mentioned earlier (see Chap. 2, Sect. 2.1.2). On the basis of the analysis conducted so far, education as a public good appears more as a static but still essential concept since it is the expression of a legislative function which mainly applies to education that is formalized and institutionalized. The concept of common good is instead dynamic and contingent. A common good is considered as such when diverse actors recognize that they have a responsibility, decide to deal with it and, therefore, to cooperate. It could therefore be argued that *formal* education constitutes a public good and this may be included in a more comprehensive approach to *education* seen as a common good. This latter could be, at the same time, the basis which inspires more participatory and democratic approaches to schooling and to higher education, and may also represent a general approach to education in both formal and non-formal contexts. Seeing education as a common good implies the development of democratic processes of participation which may be possible thanks to the empowerment of all people who are able to take responsibility and be held accountable in an integrated and humanistic approach to education.

References

Apple, M., & Beane, J. A. (1995). *Democratic Schools*. Alexandria, VA: Association for Supervision and Curriculum Development.

Apple, M., & Beane, J. A. (2007). *Democratic Schools: Lessons in Powerful Education* (2nd ed.). Portsmouth, NH: Heinemann.

Arena, G., & Iaione, C. (2012). *L'Italia dei beni comuni*. Roma: Carocci editore.

Arendt, H. (1958). *The Human Condition*. Chicago: University of Chicago Press.

Bray, M. (1999). Community Partnerships in Education: Dimensions, Variations, and Implications. *EFA Thematic Study*. The University of Hong Kong.

Bruni, L. (2012). *Le nuove virtù del mercato nell'era dei beni comuni*. Roma: Città Nuova.

Brunod, M., Moschetti, M., & Pizzardi, E. (Eds.). (2016). *La coprogettazione sociale: Esperienze, metodologie e riferimenti normativi*. Trento: Erickson.

Cahill, L. S. (2005). Globalization and the Common Good. In J. A. Coleman, W. F. Ryan, & B. Ryan (Eds.), *Globalization and Catholic Social Thought: Present Crisis, Future Hope* (pp. 42–54). Ottawa: St Paul University.

Chakroun, B., & Daelman, K. (2018). Lifelong Learning Examined from a Rights-Based Perspective: The Road Not Yet Travelled. In *The Right to Education Movements and Policies: Promises and Realities* (pp. 30–33). Norrag Special Issue 01.

Coccoli, L. (2013). Ieri, oggi, domani: i beni comuni tra passato e futuro. In L. Coccoli (Ed.), *Commons, beni comuni: il dibattito internazionale*. Meme, Collana di Filosofia.

6 Education As a Common Good   145

De Toffol, F., & Valastro, A. (2012). *Dizionario di democrazia partecipativa*. Regione Umbria: Centro Studi Politici e Giuridici.

Delors, J., et al. (1996). *Learning: The Treasure Within. Report to UNESCO of the International Commission on Education for the Twenty-first Century*. Paris: UNESCO.

Deneulin, S., & Townsend, N. (2007). Public Goods, Global Public Goods and the Common Good. *International Journal of Social Economics, 34*(1–2), 19–36.

Donati, P., & Solci, R. (2011). *I beni relazionali: che cosa sono e quali effetti producono*. Torino: Bollati Boringheri editore.

Donolo, C. (2012). I beni comuni presi sul serio. In G. Arena and C. Iaione (Eds.), *op. cit.* (pp. 13–54).

Franzini, M. (2012). I beni comuni: questioni di efficienza e di equità. In G. Arena and C. Iaione (Eds.), *op. cit.* (pp. 55–68).

Gandin, L. A., & Apple, M. W. (2002). Can Education Challenge Neo-Liberalism? The Citizen School and the Struggle for Democracy in Porto Alegre, Brazil. *Social Justice, 29*(4), 26–40.

Graebner, W. (1988). *The Engineering of Consent: Democracy as Social Authority in the Twentieth Century*. Madison: University of Wisconsin Press.

Hardin, G. (1968). The Tragedy of the Commons. *Science, New Series, 162*(3859), 1243–1248.

Hess, C., & Ostrom, E. (2007). *Understanding Knowledge as a Commons: From Theory to Practice*. The MIT Press. Retrieved from https://mitpress.mit.edu/books/understanding-knowledge-commons.

Locher, F. (2013). Cold War Pastures: Garrett Hardin and the "Tragedy of the Commons". *Revue d'histoire moderne et contemporaine, 60*(1), 7–36.

Locher, F. (2016). Third World Pastures: The Historical Roots of the Commons Paradigm (1965–1990). *Quaderni Storici, 2016*(1), 303–333.

Marginson, S. (2016). *Higher Education and the Common Good*. Melbourne: Melbourne University Publishing.

McCowan, T. (2013). *Education as a Human Right: Principles for a Universal Entitlement to Learning*. London: Bloomsbury Publishing Plc.

McCowan, T. (2016). Forging Radical Alternatives in Higher Education: The Case of Brazil. *Other Education: The Journal of Educational Alternatives, 5*(2), 196–220.

Meyer-Bisch, P., Gandolfi, S., & Balliu, G. (2016). *Souveraineté et coopérations Guide pour fonder toute gouvernance démocratique sur l'interdépendance des droits de l'homme*. Observatoire de la diversité et des droits culturels, Institut interdisciplinaire d'éthique et droits de l'homme de l'Université de Fribourg (Suisse).

Nicolas-Le Strat, P. (2015). « *Travail d'institution* » *et capacitation du commun*. Retrieved from http://blog.le-commun.fr/?p=868.

Nivarra, L. (2012). Alcune riflessioni sul rapporto fra pubblico e comune. In M. R. Marella (Ed.), *Oltre il pubblico e il privato. Per un diritto dei beni comuni* (pp. 69–87). Verona: Ombre Corte.

Ostrom, E. (1990). *Governing the Commons: The Evolution of Institutions for Collective Action*. Cambridge, UK: Cambridge University Press.

Oxfam India. (2014). *Community Participation and Institutional Experiences in School Education: School Development and Monitoring Committees in Karnataka*. New Delhi: Centre for Child and the Law National Law School of India University Bangalore.

Porter, D. O. (2012). Co-Production and Network Structures in Public Education. In V. Pestoff, T. Brandsen, & B. Verschuere (Eds.), *New Public Governance, the Third Sector and Co-Production* (pp. 145–168). New York: Routledge.

Reich, R. (2015). *Saving Capitalism: For the Many, Not the Few*. New York: Alfred Knopf.

Reimers, F. (1997). The Role of NGOs in Promoting Educational Innovation: A Case Study in Latin America. In J. Lynch, C. Modgil, & S. Modgil (Eds.), *Non-formal and Non-governmental Approaches. Vol. 4 of Education and Development: Tradition and Innovation* (pp. 33–44). London: Cassell.

Robertson, S. L. (2018). *Recovering the Political in the Idea of Education as a Public Good—And Why This Matters*. Unite for Quality Education, Blog, Education International. Retrieved from https://www.unite4education.org/global-response/recovering-the-political-in-the-idea-of-education-as-a-public-good-and-why-this-matters/.

Robeyns, I. (2017). *Wellbeing, Freedom and Social Justice: The Capability Approach Re-examined*. Cambridge: Open Book Publishers.

Rossignoli, S., & Riggall, A. (2019). *Innovation and Achievement: The Work of Four Not-for-profit School Groups*. Reading: Education Development Trust.

Shaeffer, S. (1994). *Participation for Educational Change: A Synthesis of Experience*. Paris: UNESCO International Institute for Educational Planning.

Taylor, C. (1995). *Irreducibly Social Goods. Philosophical Arguments*. Cambridge, MA: Harvard University Press.

Uemura, M. (1999). *Community Participation in Education: What Do We Know?* HDNED, The World Bank.

UNDP. (1997). *Human Development Report 1997, UNDP*. New York: Oxford University Press.

6 Education As a Common Good   147

UNESCO. (1994). *Education for All Summit of Nine High-Population Countries: Final Report.* Paris: UNESCO.

UNESCO. (2015a). *Rethinking Education: Towards a Global Common Good?* Paris: UNESCO.

UNESCO. (2015b). *Education 2030 Incheon Declaration and Framework for Action.* Paris: UNESCO.

UNESCO. (2016a, March 7). *Theme of 2017 Global Education Monitoring Report: Accountability in Education.* Concept Note. Paris: UNESCO.

UNESCO. (2016b). *Education for People and Planet: Creating Sustainable Futures for All (Global Education Monitoring Report 2016).* Paris: UNESCO.

Valastro, A. (2010). *Le regole della democrazia partecipativa: Itinerari per la costruzione di un metodo di governo.* Napoli: Jovene Editore.

Viola, F. (2012). Educare al bene comune. *Pedagogia e Vita, 70,* 181–203.

Viola, F. (2016). Beni comuni e bene comune. Paper presented at *The Issue of Common Goods: The Constitutional Perspective Conference,* La Sapienza University of Rome, 15 May 2015.

Walker, M. (2018). Dimensions of Higher Education and the Public Good in South Africa. *Higher Education, 76*(3), 555–569.

Young, I. M. (2005). Responsibility and Global Justice: A Social Connection Model. *Anales de la Cátedra Francisco Suárez, 39*(2005), 709–726.

7

Going Global: Education As a Global Common Good

It is generally accepted that the governance of education is becoming more global and therefore requires innovative principles that should result in different processes, policies and structures. By examining the literature on global governance theory, and its application to the field of education, this chapter revisits normative principles for the global governance of education. It focuses in particular on global education policy discourse and examines the concept of education as *global public goods*, as it is referred to by international actors such as the United Nations Development Programme (UNDP), the World Bank and the Education Commission. It reviews the extensive research where numerous scholars have debated the policy implications and limits of this concept as applied to education. Considering the limits of the framework of global public goods, this work analyses the extent to which the principle of education as a global *common* good may orientate the global governance of education with a view to revisiting existing hierarchies of power within global structures and to strengthening more democratic processes at a global level. This concept calls for the development of global political institutions that enable countries and their citizens to have greater voice in the decisions that affect their well-being. This approach may be relevant for

© The Author(s) 2019
R. Locatelli, *Reframing Education as a Public and Common Good*,
https://doi.org/10.1007/978-3-030-24801-7_7

149

150   R. Locatelli

the rethinking of the way international organizations and aid agencies involved in education function. It may also encourage the diversity of approaches while countering dominant development discourse, characterized by the primacy of economics and by a more instrumental vision of education.

7.1 The Governance of Education in an Increasingly Complex Global Context

The global education commitment, which was renewed in 2015 with the adoption of the Education 2030 agenda, represents for many countries and for the international community both an extraordinary opportunity and a significant challenge. Despite substantial efforts made by many countries and donors, over the last five years, the number of out-of-school children has remained unvaried (UIS and UNESCO 2016). As mentioned in Chap. 4, it is estimated that in 2017, 9 per cent of children worldwide, corresponding to 64 million children, still did not have access to primary education (UNESCO 2018). The figures referring to out-of-school children and teenagers are even more staggering if we consider the commitment envisaged in the new Sustainable Development Goal 4 (SDG4) for education, Target 4.1, which commits governments to "ensure that all girls and boys complete free, equitable and quality primary *and* secondary education"[1] (emphasis added). Despite this ambitious commitment, according to recent data of the UNESCO (United Nations Educational, Scientific and Cultural Organization) Institute for Statistics, of the 262 million children and teenagers out of school in 2017, 61 million (16 per cent) are of lower secondary school age, and 138 million (36 per cent) of upper secondary (UNESCO 2018). It has been argued that the goal of the new education target looks unrealistic, especially with regard to upper secondary education for all (UNESCO 2015a). It is estimated that to achieve this goal by 2030, US$39 billion will be needed every year to fill the funding gap in low

---

[1] SDG4, Target 4.1: By 2030, ensure that all girls and boys complete free, equitable and quality primary and secondary education leading to relevant and effective learning outcomes (UN 2015).

7 Going Global: Education As a Global Common Good 151

and lower middle-income countries (UIS and UNESCO 2016). At current progress rates, however, countries worldwide will ensure universal primary education only by 2042; lower secondary education by 2059, and upper secondary education only by 2084 (UNESCO 2016). Moreover, there were about 750 million illiterate adults in 2017. The global adult literacy rate was 86 per cent but only 65 per cent in sub-Saharan Africa (UNESCO 2018). While the total number of illiterate young people fell from 144 million in 2000 to 102 million in 2017, the number of illiterates over age 65 is continuing to rise. In 2016, there were 40 per cent more illiterate elderly than illiterate youth (UNESCO 2018).

Moreover, according to the International Commission on Financing Global Education Opportunity, by 2030 half a generation or 800 million out of 1.6 billion children will not have the skills to enter the world of work. The majority of them will live in low and middle-income countries, where it is estimated that only one in 10 young people will have the basic skills needed for a successful future (Education Commission 2016). Domestic resources will be necessary to deal with this funding gap and in many countries "annual total expenditure would need to more than double from current levels, and some countries would need to increase expenditure considerably more than that" (UNESCO 2015a: 294). Moreover, mobilization of domestic resources will have to be complemented by strong measures against phenomena of corruption and of inefficient spending of public money (UNESCO 2015a). As indicated by the Education Commission, attention to performance, innovation and inclusion should also encourage an increase in public national resources.

A recent report of the UN Interagency Task Force on Financing for Development affirms that "[a]chieving SDG 4 on quality education for all requires significant additional financing. Annual total spending to achieve the first two—and costliest—education targets, namely universal pre-primary, primary and secondary education, would need to more than triple in low-income countries" (UN 2019: xx)[2]. However, domestic resources alone will not be sufficient to reach the basic education target by 2030. It

---

[2] UN. (2019). *Financing for Sustainable Development Report 2019*. Inter-agency Task Force on Financing for Development, New York: United Nations. Available at: https://developmentfinance. un.org/fsdr2019.

152   R. Locatelli

is estimated that, with regard to basic education, annual external financing should be around $US22 billion from 2015 to 2030. However, over the past decade, education has become less of a priority for development partners, with the share of education falling from 8.8 per cent of total Official Development Assistance (ODA) in 2010 to 7.1 per cent in 2017 (UN 2019). It is estimated that this funding gap will widen further (UNESCO 2015a) and, according to recent trends of aid flows, the total aid to education will level off in the coming years, with poor countries being mostly affected (GCE 2013). Moreover, the share of aid allocated to education among multilateral organizations such as the World Bank, the African Development Fund and the Asian Development Bank has decreased over the last ten years. Aid allocated to the education sector represented 10 per cent in the 2002–2004 biennium, while in that of 2012–2014 it was only 7 per cent.[3] Within this context, for the education 4.1 target to be achieved by 2030, education as a sector has to be prioritized both within domestic public expenditure as well as within external aid allocation.

New financing mechanisms need to be identified (UNESCO 2015a). Here, the role of non-state actors such as NGOs and the private sector could be of help as long as the State ensures that the concept of education as a public good is not undermined. In view of this, the idea that education should be funded and managed entirely by the State is neither feasible nor desirable (Rizvi 2016). While it is widely agreed that the primary responsibility for funding, delivering and monitoring education lies at the national level,[4] it is also increasingly acknowledged that States operate within networks. The way of functioning of the traditional welfare state is increasingly called into question by the emergence of new governance arrangements and mechanisms at local, regional and global levels. It has been argued that we are witnessing the emergence of a new form of Network State (Carnoy and Castells 2001):

> It is a state made of shared institutions, and enacted by bargaining and interactive iteration all along the chain of decision making: national

---

[3] Data presented by The International Commission on Financing Global Education Opportunity during the Webinar #5, held on 2 August 2016.

[4] *Incheon Declaration and Education 2030 Framework for Action. Towards inclusive and equitable quality education and lifelong learning for all* (UNESCO, 2015c).

governments, co-national governments, supra-national bodies, international institutions, governments of nationalities, regional governments, local governments, and NGOs (...). Decision-making and representation take place all along the chain, not necessarily in the hierarchical, prescripted order. This new state functions as a network, in which all nodes interact, and are equally necessary for the performance of the state's functions. The state of the Information Age is a Network State. (p. 14)

In this increasingly complex context, it is necessary to examine how education governance has evolved and the implications with regard to the multiple processes of education decision-making at a global level.

7.1.1 The Implications of Globalization on the Governance of Education

The provision of numerous goods and services relies increasingly on the implementation of international policies able to address the needs of different peoples, particularly in the case of education. As aforementioned, the education sector received consistent attention at the international level with the recognition of education as a human right and as a main driver for socio-economic development. Moreover, the considerable expansion of educational opportunities worldwide, together with the demographic growth, has created opportunities for non-state actors to get involved in the sector. As a result, "systems of norm-setting and regulation in the delivery of global goods such as education [...] are becoming more complex" (UNESCO 2015b: 67). Beyond inter-governmental organizations, the involvement of non-state actors at the global level also includes international civil society organizations, transnational corporations, foundations and think tanks. These actors inevitably influence and orientate, either directly or indirectly, national education policy formulation through the setting of global agendas, international aid assistance, loans provision or capacity development. The emergence of a global level of educational policy and practice can be traced back to "the context of larger trends of economic and cultural convergence collectively referred to as globalization" (Shields 2013: 117).

Globalization is commonly referred to as a set of processes of intensification of interdependence, interconnection, relationships and exchanges of capital, goods, information, ideas and people across the world (Solesin 2018). Since the 1990s, the processes of globalization and the shifting dynamics of international education development have drastically transformed the landscape of education governance. This transformation is characterized by the emergence of multiple sources of decision-making alongside and beyond nation-states, which affect and influence the way education systems are governed. Globalization has resulted in greater economic integration and in the narrowing perception of the purposes of education; it has undoubtedly accelerated digital connectivity, with an impact on the content, processes and organization of learning, thus also contributing to the convergence towards a global cultural model, in education too. It is also having an impact on how social spaces are organized, leading to the strengthening of social connections beyond the geographical national boundaries (Solesin 2018). In the field of education, globalization is most apparent in the convergence of education systems around a common "international model" of policies and practices, which is sometimes referred to as *isomorphism* (Meyer et al. 1997). Public education systems worldwide are fundamentally organized in a similar way: they are "coordinated by a central ministry of education and delivered through a system of schools. Internally, schools are organized into classrooms that are led by certified professional teachers. Students study a standard curriculum that varies little according to their own national and cultural context" (Shields 2013: 62–63).

It is within this context of globalization that there has been a shift in the dynamics of international cooperation in education. Education policy and practice are increasingly conceptualized and enacted on a global or international level. From the expansion of basic education to emerging trends in higher education, policies and practices are no longer solely determined by autonomous governments acting independently. Instead, global initiatives—Education for All (EFA) Movement and SDGs—result from complex processes of negotiation and influence involving a web of actors at the global, regional, national and local levels. This global level of educational activity has emerged over the course of many decades and was first evident within the international development sector fol-

7 Going Global: Education As a Global Common Good   155

lowing the Second World War. The shifting dynamics of international cooperation in education are characterized by the emergence of education multilateralism, the creation of global agendas and goals, as well as by changing patterns of public and private financing of education (Shields 2013).

Educational activity on the global level accelerated with the adoption of the first international Education for All agenda in 1990. International mechanisms for financing education were also established, and non-state involvement in the funding, provision and management of education were encouraged, thus reshaping traditional roles in education governance. The shifting dynamics of international cooperation in education in the context of globalization have modified the structures, actors and processes that define the governance of education (Solesin 2018). It follows that the governance of education cannot be reduced to the governance at the national level. A broader approach to governance is required in order to consider how different actors involved in education interact at the national and international level. Education policies and priorities are now being negotiated and defined both inside and outside the Ministry of Education, and the decisions made at the national level might have global repercussions. Along these lines, Solesin (2018) defines the global governance of education

> as a methodological and theoretical framework which highlights the broader global space in which governance in education now happens. Global governance of education defines and entails all processes and structures for exercising power and authority in order to steer and influence education in the global[…]. All education stakeholders, regardless of their status (private or public) and level (local or international), can be actors of global governance of education. (p. 28)

Global governance of education involves the circulation of global policy discourses, the definition of educational purposes, the management and delivery of private education opportunities, as well as the establishment of global policy priorities. It is evident that these trends "have made the national characterisation of public goods somewhat limited" since the formulation of education policy is progressively shifting from the State to the global level (Menashy 2009: 310).

7.2 From Global Public Goods to Global Common Goods

Some have suggested that the framework of *global public goods* may represent an attempt to capture the complex dynamics that have repercussions on the production of goods and may therefore provide useful guidance for their governance. Mostly referred to by international organizations such as the United Nations Development Programme (UNDP), the World Bank and the Education Commission (2016) the framework of global public goods is grounded on a revisited theory of public goods, in particular of the concept of *publicness*[5]. This is based on the acknowledgment of a greater concern for the public sphere among the main actors involved in policy issues—the State, business, civil society organizations and households—which has led to an "expansion of the public domain" (Drache 2001; Kaul and Mendoza 2003).

It was in the perspective of rethinking the definition of public goods to make it more relevant to the changing global dynamics, that in 1999, the UNDP outlined a landmark publication by Kaul, Grunberg and Stern. The authors recognize the need to reframe the role of the State both within its interaction with non-State actors but also in terms of its geographical and jurisdictional dimensions. Global public goods are therefore defined as public goods which are global in their benefits, be it by nature or by political choice (Kaul and Mendoza 2003). Global public goods have been defined as "outcomes (or intermediate products) that tend towards universality in the sense that they benefit all countries, population groups, and generations" (Kaul et al. 1999: 16). This definition means that, in contrast to economic theory, the concept of "goods", as reconstructed by Kaul et al. includes a large spectrum of global issues such as climate change mitigation, financial stability, international security, knowledge production and global public health. The term "global public goods" has therefore "gradually become a buzzword in the global

---

[5] According to Kaul, Grunberg and Stern, the characterization of the *publicness* or *privateness* dimension of a certain good involves the general public and political process. The "triangle of publicness" includes *publicness* in decision-making, in consumption and in the distribution of benefits (Kaul and Mendoza 2003).

policy discourse, evolving from a technical, economic concept to a powerful means of increasing public awareness in favour of greater international cooperation and regulation in today's globalized world" (Cogolati and Wouters 2018: 8).

However, some authors have argued that the concept of global public goods, and hence of education as a global public good, may prove to be ineffective for the regulation of privatization policies (Menashy 2009). According to Dardot and Laval (2014), this theory would have the virtue to depoliticize the issue of public goods and neglect the conflicts among social and economic powers, assuming that they represent only technical or strategic problems. Indeed, the global public goods' theory appears to be designed to promote more cooperation among existing private and state actors and to justify a return to old public or private institutions which do not afford communities the same right to participate and shape their own process of development (Dardot 2018). As argued by Menashy, "global public goods policies potentially perpetuate the harmful facets of economic globalization via the spread of capitalism" (2009: 316). Since this theory does not call into question the intrinsic characteristics of economic globalization, it may result ineffective in counterbalancing the negative effects of the diffusion of globalization itself. In particular, northern bilateral agencies and international organizations will probably set the agenda for the production of global public goods, perpetuating a "subtle form of conditionality" (Carbone 2007). The framework of global public goods would only replicate the state of international cooperation, characterized by oligopolistic competition, where the number of actors able to significantly influence strategic policies is very small (Coussy 2005).

At this time of ever-increasing conflicts and widening gaps of inequality worldwide, there is a need to strengthen a humanistic and universal perspective on education. The concept of *global common goods* implies commitment to a community that is both universal in scope and that takes the differences among peoples and cultures with the full seriousness they deserve (Hollenbach 2002). This is all the more necessary for the provision of constructive alternatives and creative responses to the challenges that arise from the crisis of the current economic model, in order to mitigate the perverse effects of globalization on social justice and equity. A humanistic approach that "should support the development of

158   R. Locatelli

a person into a human being"[6] and should inspire a democratic governance of education, at both the national and global level, that enables us to think in terms of shared responsibility. In other words, the perspective is the realization of the human-being which entails everyone's responsibility with regard to development of the people of one's community, as well as of the people of the world.

Although both the global public good and the global common good approaches touch on the issue of the shortcomings of collective action, include a global dimension and overlap partly with regard to the goods to which they apply, they put an emphasis on different policy instruments, advocate distinct governance mechanisms and carry a different set of political, economic and legal implications. Above all, they put forward contrasting views on the role of the State, multilateral organizations and international law. Indeed, the concept of global common goods, as opposed to that of global public goods, implies a different model of governance, a system of bottom-up governance alternative to that of the traditional market-state dichotomy. While the governance of global common goods cannot be dissociated from bottom-up management practices and relies on a decentralized decision-making process that turns the community of the stakeholders into an independent self-governing body, the governance of global public goods "presupposes a high degree of centralization of the decision-making process [...] with the monitoring of the compliance of all actors" (Deleixhe 2018: 331). To be both efficient and legitimate, the governance of global common goods should not strive for the integration of its different international regimes into a single scheme but rather improve their interrelation and increase their overlap, thus creating a stronger polycentric governance.

The governance of global common goods seems therefore to offer a more promising model for an effective and legitimate global governance than that of global public goods. Not that the latter cannot be effective, but its organizational mode is closer to a single world-state than to a polycentric federalism (Deleixhe 2018). Indeed, global common goods, just as governance, depend on a decentralized scheme of cooperation and

---

[6] Jacques Maritain quoted in Elfert (2015).

cannot operate if stakeholders do not consent to the social rules they must observe, whereas global public goods respond to a logic of government, since they require a strong centralized authority. This entails new forms of international cooperation, grounded on a new culture of solidarity, able to address "globalization's democratic deficit" (Nye 2001).

7.3 Education As a Global Common Good: Towards New Forms of International Cooperation

Recognizing the international dimensions of education, this book recognizes the concept of education as a global common good as a useful framework for the governance of education in the global context. Indeed, education is a process which is essential to the development of people in every part of the world, and its fulfilment should be in the interest of both local/national well-being and that of the global community. This vision emphasizes education as a common right and a growing necessity and source of global understanding (Marginson 2018). The notion of education as a global common good calls for the development of global political institutions and methods of governance that enable countries and their citizens to have a greater say in the decisions that affect their well-being. This is necessary to encourage the diversity of approaches while countering dominant development discourse, characterized by a more instrumental vision of education. Moreover, especially in countries affected by conflict, in a state of emergency, or in very poor conditions, where people's safety and survival represent the priority of any intervention, the responsibility with regard to education should be assumed by those actors who can take charge of it. This is why the responsibility has to be universal[7] if it is not to undermine the possibility for all children, no matter where, to have the opportunity for education.

---

[7] The expression "Universal Responsibility" has been used by the Director of the Swiss Agency for Development and Cooperation in the editorial "La responsabilité est désormais partagée" in *Un seul monde*, n.1, February 2016. www.eda.admin.ch/deza/fr/home/publications-services/publications/series-publications/un-seul-monde.html/content/publikationen/fr/deza/eine-welt/eine-welt-1-2016.

160   R. Locatelli

Conceiving education as a global common good implies a renewed form of cooperation among political institutions involved in education policy formulation and practice at the global level, which should promote "participation of all peoples in a diverse and differentiated, yet solidaristic and collaborative, world society" (Cahill 2005: 54). The democratic governance of education at the global level can be fostered thanks to efforts of international organizations, both in their collaboration with nation-states and within the partnerships realized with other stakeholders such as international civil society organizations, indigenous communities, philanthropic groups. Indeed, education has always been a fundamental domain of cooperation. Cooperation, equity and inclusion, opposed to individualism based on competition are fundamental principles that characterize global common goods. International institutions have, however, different approaches to education, and this is reflected in the policies that they implement in several countries worldwide.[8] In this respect, it is important to highlight that privatization policies that lead to the consideration of education as an individual marketable, consumable good, are in sharp contradiction with the conception of education as a global common good. For these reasons, the influence of international organizations on the convergence of education systems towards a common set of policies and practices needs to be examined (Shields 2013).

7.3.1   Partnerships: For Cooperation, Not "For Profit"

Within global governance arrangements, innovative solutions which involve greater participation of different stakeholders should be developed in order to meet the current challenges of financing, quality and equity. Given the right conditions, partnerships between communities, States, international bodies and other non-state actors may provide adequate opportunities both to complement the current functions and role of the State and to develop stronger education systems especially in those

---

[8] For a detailed analysis of the World Bank policies and strategies in education, see Klees, Samoff and Stromquist (2012).

7 Going Global: Education As a Global Common Good 161

contexts where the capacity and the financial opportunities of States need to be improved and supported. A vision of partnership inspired by the words of Jacques Delors who, in 1996, suggested that international cooperation should be seen in the context of partnership rather than aid:

> [E]xperience militates in favour of partnerships, globalization makes it inescapable, and there are some encouraging examples such as the successful co-operation and exchanges within regional groupings. (…) Another justification for partnership is that it can lead to a 'win-win situation': whilst industrialized countries can assist developing countries by the input of their successful experiences, their technologies and financial and material resources, they can learn from the developing countries ways of passing on their cultural heritage, approaches to the socialization of children and, more fundamentally, different cultures and ways of life. (1996: 34)

The State, with the support of international organizations, where necessary, may consider the establishment of partnerships as an opportunity to increase the availability of funds and provisions in order to develop a strong educational system of good quality, available to all. According to the UNESCO Global Education Monitoring Report (2016), partnerships are necessary if the ambitious targets of the SDGs are to be achieved. Indeed, there is growing recognition that all actors need to plan together, act together and commit to equity and sustainability. Within partnership arrangements, potential roles should be specifically designed for civil society, the private sector and other non-state actors in the financing and implementation in a framework of mutual accountability. As recalled in the Global Education Monitoring (GEM) Report, some factors—including securing high level leadership, context-specific and country-led partnerships, clarity of role and responsibilities—focus on financing, results and accountability, are determinant in making development partnerships effective (UNESCO 2016). The Education Commission also considers partnerships with non-state actors at both the national and global level as a tool for innovation in order to build successful education systems: "there is great potential for a diverse set of organizations from every sector to help expand and improve education if partnered and regulated effectively by governments"

(Education Commission 2016). The commission urges governments "to strengthen their capacity to harness the potential of all partners. In particular, this should include improving the regulation of non-state providers of education in order to enhance their contributions and protect rights".

These partnerships may be established at the local level and may enhance community participation. With regard to this, it is widely acknowledged that the work of many civil society organizations and grass-roots initiatives by non-governmental organizations, of social and cultural actors at the local and global level, may actually result in an increase in awareness about certain educational issues, thus promoting community engagement and educational quality. If social and cultural actors had greater access to information and involvement in decision-making, it may encourage greater relevance of education pedagogy and curriculum to local needs. Partnerships with local communities and civil society may enhance transparency and therefore the evaluation of the education system, thus sustaining the quality of the work and the accountability of public authorities against the risk of corruption and inefficiency (UNESCO 2015a).

In the context of partnerships, however, particular attention should be given to the arrangements increasingly referred to as Public–Private Partnerships (PPPs). As above discussed, it is argued that these partnerships very often contemplate the involvement of private, international corporate for-profit actors which directly or indirectly enhance a vision of education as a private, consumable, marketable good. Therefore, instead of constituting stimulating governance arrangements, partnerships of this kind may weaken the role of the State as a guarantor of the public sphere. It follows that, with regard to PPPs, "[t]he original sense of partnership (…) needs to be the standard of measurement. This assumption needs to be tested against reality in each case" (Draxler 2012: 46). Knowing that PPPs cannot be treated as a homogeneous phenomenon, there is a need to assess, case by case, how these partnerships function, how they are structured, and what implications they have for neo-liberal globalization and democratization (Ginsburg 2012: 75). As clearly suggested by Draxler (2012), "PPPs can provide an exciting laboratory to test new tools and pedagogy, to implement management reform, to

7 Going Global: Education As a Global Common Good   163

diversify the types of education on offer, and to involve new partners. But proper planning, clarity about purpose, ensuring equity, care for cost-benefit and scalability, democratic process, evaluation and sustainability remain the foundation stones of any serious education initiative" (2012: 58). Indeed, however limited favouring public–private partnerships may be, the trend is undeniable (Minow 2003). Sceptics should not simply decry this reality but deal with it by demanding public accountability at both national and international level.

Partnerships among countries and other regional, international and multilateral organizations may also represent useful arrangements for financial and technical support to the development of public education systems. In this respect, the Global Partnership for Education (GPE), formerly known as the *Education for All - Fast Track Initiative*, launched in 2002 to accelerate progress towards the goal of universal completion of quality primary education by 2015, aims at intensifying support to governments in order to strengthen public education systems in those developing countries which are partners of the GPE. This partnership brings together donor countries, developing countries as well as regional, bilateral and multilateral agencies and organizations and a wide range of national, regional and global civil society networks, teacher associations, foundations and corporations. The Global Partnership operates both globally and locally. Globally, the partnership "engages with the education community worldwide as a convener and consensus-broker and as an advocate for key priorities on the path to achieving universal high-quality basic education". Locally, the GPE supplies technical and financial assistance to developing countries. In contrast to recent trends which have witnessed the decline of Official Development Assistance (ODA) in education in the last decades, the GPE is creating the opportunities and capacities for developing country partners to improve their public education systems. Indeed, it is estimated that, on average, the domestic expenditure on education, as a share of GDP in developing country partners, was 10 per cent greater after the countries joined the partnership (GPE 2013).

The Global Education Monitoring Report (UNESCO 2016) also identifies the Education 2030 coordination structures as "Global

164   R. Locatelli

Multistakeholder Partnerships in Education", given their crucial role in coordinating the activities towards the achievement of SDG 4. In particular, the Steering Committee is expected to bring coherence in the Education 2030 activities since it is expected to be the main mechanism in supporting countries, reviewing progress and encouraging harmonization and coordination of partner activities.

7.3.2   The Role of International Organizations

The concept of common goods, unlike that of the *commons*, requires public institutions to play a crucial role in their governance. In the same way, the concept of global common goods also requires international public institutions to assume responsibility for the democratic governance of education at the global level. Indeed, education cannot be treated as any other global commons such as oceans, the atmosphere and outer space, since it cannot be referred to as a natural resource but rather as a process through which human beings can evolve, or with regard to formal education, as a social function which translates into the availability of educational opportunities at different levels. In this respect, the governance of education in a global context requires international organizations to promote forms of international cooperation inspired by principles of solidarity, social justice, inclusion and public accountability.

In this respect, the aim of UNESCO is specifically that of implementing international cooperation in education, science and culture, "in a spirit of mutual assistance and concern" (Preamble of the UNESCO constitution). Education is considered by the founders of UNESCO as "a means to achieve the unity of 'humanity' and foster better understanding of different peoples, as a pre-condition for peace in a globalizing world" (Elfert 2015: p. 2). UNESCO, within its norm-setting role, as well as leading the coordination of the global Education 2030 agenda, is in a privileged position regarding the governance of education as a global common good. Notably, the mandate of this UN agency is "to give every man living his chance to help make humanity more conscious of its unity"[9]. In

---

[9] Georges Bidault quoted in Elfert (2015)

7 Going Global: Education As a Global Common Good 165

> ### The Education 2030 Framework for Action
>
> The Education 2030 Framework for Action, adopted in 2015 at the World Education Forum (Incheon, Republic of Korea), contains important elements that draw on the direction as framed by the concept of education as a global common good. While recognizing that the State is the main duty bearer and "its role is essential in setting and regulating standards and norms", it is also acknowledged that "[c]ivil society, teachers and educators, the private sector, communities, families, youth and children all have important roles in realizing the right to quality education." (UNESCO 2015c: 10). Among the several implementation modalities related to "Governance, accountability and partnerships" of the new agenda, the participation of communities is considered as an essential tool to "boost transparency and to guarantee good governance in the education administration" (UNESCO 2015c: 79).
>
> Moreover, one of the indicative strategies necessary to reach Target 4.1[10] considers the greater involvement of communities, including young people and parents, in the management of schools as essential for strengthening "the efficiency and effectiveness of institutions, school leadership and governance" (UNESCO 2015c: 34).
>
> In line with the need to ensure an integrated and holistic approach to education as a common good, the indicative strategies related to the means of implementation related to Target 4.a[11] also suggest that "learning spaces and environments for non-formal and adult learning and education, [...] including networks of community learning centres and spaces" should be made widely available (UNESCO 2015c: 66).

this respect, the humanistic and universal vision can be realized in "making of education a universal message in order to try, not to unify this world, but to bring together the different parties in their diversity, which means to accept the difference and to respect the other" (Delors and Arnaud 2004: 441; translated by Elfert 2015).

International organizations such as UNESCO should support States in the implementation of education as a common good at the national

---

[10] Target 4.1: "By 2030, ensure that all girls and boys complete free, equitable and quality primary and secondary education leading to relevant and effective learning outcomes"

[11] Target 4.a: "Build and upgrade education facilities that are child-, disability- and gender-sensitive and provide safe, non-violent, inclusive and effective learning environments for all".

level, allowing the participation and inclusion of different actors in a democratic process of policy formulation and implementation. At the same time, international organizations should be democratic in their own ways of functioning if they are to promote democracy in the governance of education at the global level. The mechanisms designed to monitor and steer the implementation of the global education agenda have represented an attempt to enhance democratic governance, as embodied in the principle of education as a global common good. Indeed, the Incheon Declaration affirms that the commitment towards Education 2030 represents a collective and shared responsibility. This is particularly relevant especially when considering the global governance of education. Indeed, "whereas governments can function even in the face of widespread opposition to their policies", governance presupposes an element of deliberate cooperation, since it relies on the consent of its participants (Deleixhe 2018: 331).

The coordination mechanisms established by UNESCO reflect the variety of actors involved in education at the global level. Since 2012, the steering committees convened by UNESCO have represented the most important mechanisms for the provision of strategic guidance and support in the implementation of the education global agendas. In particular, the new Global Education 2030 Steering Committee established by the Framework for Action (UNESCO 2015c) is composed of 38 members representing a majority from Member States of all UNESCO regional groups, as well as co-convening agencies (UNICEF, UNDP, UNFPA, UNHCR, UNWOMEN, ILO, World Bank), Organization for Economic Cooperation and Development and Global Partnership for Education, regional organizations, teacher organizations and civil society networks. In addition, a rotating group of affiliated members, including representatives of the private sector, foundations, youth and student organizations was also established. The composition of the Steering Committee reflects the central role that Member States play in the formulation of strategies and recommendations to implement education policies at the global level.[12]

---

[12] Moreover, Member States have played a central role also in the development and adoption of the 2030 Agenda for Sustainable Development, taking distance from the top-down process that characterized the adoption of the Millennium Development goals Agenda.

7 Going Global: Education As a Global Common Good   167

Having said this, it is also important to bear in mind that institutions such as UNESCO, which embody world culture values, may also be susceptible to influence from economic interests that seek to redefine these values in a way that serves their purposes. Independent analysis of social relationships of power should be dealt with closely also by international organizations. If integrated educational work on a global level is to continue, development of critical consciousness through education, even within international organizations, "is a vital necessity and a worthy goal" (Shields 2013: 120).

The efforts towards achieving more democratic processes which have been developing in the last few years represent an important attempt to give voice to various actors and promote a common vision and commitment to education. It has been argued that there is still need for "increased transparency and commitment to democratic governance linked to decision making processes within the EFA architecture, to ensure that decisions resulting from such processes be fully respected"[13]. This is necessary to guarantee that different voices and representations of worldviews, of conceptions of development and of well-being, are seriously taken into account and can have an influence in the formulation of policies. Indeed, partnerships for the realization of the new global education agenda should be based on this humanistic, and universal, vision of education as a global common good. The concept of "global common goods" is more inclusive and allows for rethinking our approach to education in the face of various cultural traditions across the world in an increasingly changing landscape. Everyone through education can develop those universal values which include respect for life and human dignity, equal rights and social justice, cultural diversity, international solidarity and shared responsibility.

---

[13] Collective Consultation of NGOs on Education for All. (2014). Final Declaration: *Realizing the Right to Education Beyond 2015*. Seventh Meeting of the CCNGO/EFA - Santiago, Chile, 21–23 May 2014.

References

Cahill, L. S. (2005). Globalization and the Common Good. In J. A. Coleman & W. F. Ryan (Eds.), *Globalization and Catholic Social Thought: Present Crisis, Future Hope* (pp. 42–54). Ottawa: St Paul University.

Carbone, M. (2007). Supporting or Resisting Global Public Goods? The Policy Dimension of a Contested Concept. *Global Governance, 13*, 179–198.

Carnoy, M., & Castells, M. (2001). Globalization, the Knowledge Society, and the Network State: Poulantzas at the Millennium. *Global Networks, 1*(1), 1–18.

Cogolati, S., & Wouters, J. (Eds.). (2018). *The Commons and a New Global Governance* (Leuven Global Governance Series). Cheltenham: Edward Elgar Publishing Limited.

Coussy, J. (2005). The Adventures of a Concept: Is Neo-classical Theory Suitable for Defining Global Public Goods? *Review of International Political Economy, 12*(1), 177–194.

Dardot, P. (2018). What Democracy for the Global Commons? In S. Cogolati & J. Wouters (Eds.), *The Commons and a New Global Governance (20–36)* (Leuven Global Governance Series). Cheltenham: Edward Elgar Publishing Limited.

Dardot, P., & Laval, C. (2014). *Commun: Essai sur la révolution au XXIe siècle.* Paris: La Découverte.

Deleixhe, M. (2018). Conclusion: Is the Governance of the Commons a Model for a New Global Governance? In S. Cogolati & J. Wouters (Eds.), *The Commons and a New Global Governance (322–334)* (Leuven Global Governance Series). Cheltenham: Edward Elgar Publishing Limited.

Delors, J., & Arnaud, J.-L. (2004). *Mémoires.* Paris: Plon.

Delors, J., et al. (1996). *Learning: The Treasure Within. Report to UNESCO of the International Commission on Education for the Twenty-first Century.* Paris: UNESCO.

Drache, D. (2001). *The Market or the Public Domain? Global Governance and the Asymmetry of Power.* London: Routledge.

Draxler, A. (2012). International PPPs in Education: New Potential or Privatizing Public Goods? In S. L. Robertson, K. Mundy, A. Verger, & F. Menashy (Eds.), *Public Private Partnerships in Education: New Actors and Modes of Governance in a Globalizing World* (pp. 43–62). Cheltenham: Edward Elgar.

7 Going Global: Education As a Global Common Good 169

Education Commission. (2016). *The Learning Generation: Investing in Education for a Changing World*. The International Commission on Financing Global Education Opportunity.

Elfert, M. (2015). *Learning to Live Together: Revisiting the Humanism of the Delors Report* (*ERF Working Papers Series*, No. 12). Paris: UNESCO Education Research and Foresight.

GCE. (2013). *Education Aid Watch 2013*. Johannesburg, South Africa: Global Campaign for Education.

Ginsburg, M. (2012). Public Private Partnerships, Neoliberal Globalization and Democratization. In S. L. Robertson, K. Mundy, A. Verger, & F. Menashy (Eds.), *Public Private Partnerships in Education: New Actors and Modes of Governance in a Globalizing World* (pp. 63–78). Cheltenham: Edward Elgar.

GPE. (2013). *Facing the Challenges of Data, Financing and Fragility: Results for Learning Report 2013*. Washington, DC: Global Partnership for Education.

Hollenbach, D. (2002). *The Global Common Good*. Cambridge: Cambridge University Press.

Kaul, I., & Mendoza, R. U. (2003). Advancing the Concept of Public Goods. In I. Kaul, P. Conceicao, K. Le Goulven, & R. U. Mendoza (Eds.), *Providing Global Public Goods: Managing Globalization* (pp. 78–111). New York: United Nations Development Programme.

Kaul, I., Grunberg, I., & Stern, M. A. (1999). *Global Public Goods: International Cooperation in the 21st Century*. New York: United Nations Development Programme.

Klees, S., Samoff, J., & Stromquist, N. P. (Eds.). (2012). *The World Bank and Education: Critiques and Alternatives*. Rotterdam: Sense Publishers.

Marginson, S. (2018). Higher Education as a Global Common Good. *International Association of Universities IAU Horizons, 23*(2), 17–18.

Menashy, F. (2009). Education as a Global Public Good: The Applicability and Implications of a Framework. *Globalisation, Societies and Education, 7*(3), 307–320.

Meyer, J., Boli, J., Thomas, G., & Ramirez, F. (1997). World Society and the Nation-State. *American Journal of Sociology, 103*(1), 144–181. https://doi.org/10.1086/231174.

Minow, M. (2003). Public and Private Partnerships: Accounting for the New Religion. *Harvard Law Review, 116*(5), 1229–1270.

Nye, J. S., Jr. (2001). Globalization's Democratic Deficit: How to Make International Institutions More Accountable. *Foreign Affairs, 80*(4), 2–6.

Rizvi, F. (2016). *Privatization in Education: Trends and Consequences* (*ERF Working Papers Series*, 18). Paris: UNESCO.

Shields, R. (2013). *Globalization and International Education*, Contemporary Issues in Education Studies, Bloomsbury Publishing Plc.

Solesin, L. (2018). *The Role of UNESCO in the Global Governance of Education*. PhD Thesis, Doctoral Degree in Intercultural Humanistic Studies, University of Bergamo.

UIS and UNESCO. (2016). *Leaving No One Behind: How Far on the Way to Universal Primary and Secondary Education?* (*Policy Paper 27/ Fact Sheet 37*). Paris: UNESCO.

UN. (2015). *Transforming Our World: The 2030 Agenda for Sustainable Development*. New York: United Nations. (UN General Assembly Resolution 70/1.).

UN. (2019). *Financing for Sustainable Development Report 2019*. Inter-agency Task Force on Financing for Development, New York: United Nations. https://developmentfinance.un.org/fsdr2019.

UNESCO. (2015a). *Education for All 2000–2015 – Achievements and Challenges* (*EFA Global Monitoring Report 2015*). Paris: UNESCO.

UNESCO. (2015b). *Rethinking Education: Towards a Global Common Good?* Paris: UNESCO.

UNESCO. (2015c). *Education 2030 Incheon Declaration and Framework for Action*. Paris: UNESCO.

UNESCO. (2016). *Education for People and Planet: Creating Sustainable Futures for All* (*Global Education Monitoring Report 2016*). Paris: UNESCO.

UNESCO. (2018). *Migration, Displacement and Education: Building Bridges, Not Walls* (*Global Education Monitoring Report 2019*). Paris: UNESCO.

8

Conclusion

Over the last two decades, access to education has expanded at all levels at unprecedented rates, especially at the primary level, resulting in the positive reduction of the number of out-of-school children and adolescents by almost half since 2000 (UNESCO 2015a). This remarkable progress is due in part to the Education for All and Millennium Development Goals global agendas which have put greater emphasis on the need to ensure education for all, especially at the basic and compulsory levels.

However, despite this significant expansion of access to formal education, the target of universal primary education has not yet been reached. Too many children still remain out-of-school worldwide and the most underprivileged continue to be the least likely to be able to access education. The situation is particularly alarming in countries at war and in fragile countries where the share of out-of-school children is most concentrated. In particular, the education needs of the most vulnerable people in the world, such as minorities, indigenous communities, migrants, refugees and internally displaced people are often unmet, with marginalization resulting as an impediment to building more inclusive and resilient societies (UNESCO 2018).

© The Author(s) 2019 **171**
R. Locatelli, *Reframing Education as a Public and Common Good,*
https://doi.org/10.1007/978-3-030-24801-7_8

172   R. Locatelli

These trends have come hand in hand with a "progressive acknowledgment of the alarming scale of the quality deficit" which has led to a shift in global discussions from a traditional focus on access to a greater concern for the learning actually taking place (UNESCO 2015a: 13). According to estimates from the UNESCO (United Nations Educational, Scientific and Cultural Organization) Institute for Statistics (UIS), more than 617 million children and adolescents are not achieving minimum proficiency levels in reading and mathematics. In addition, despite the steady rise in literacy rates over the past 50 years, there are still 750 million illiterate adults around the world, most of whom are women (UIS database). If properly designed and monitored, education technologies may represent useful tools to improve literacy and learning outcomes, but they can also lead to the risk of "exacerbating inequalities, promoting superficial learning, and burdening education ministries especially in low and middle-income countries with expensive and useless equipment".[1]

As investigated throughout this book, the growing demand for education, also resulting from the significant demographic changes occurring worldwide, has placed greater pressure on public financing, already constrained by the global economic and financial crisis of 2008 (UNESCO 2015b). The trends of privatization and marketization are in part the result of the educational crisis affecting countries both in the global North and in the global South, and of the failure of governments to provide basic education of quality for all. The global Education 2030 agenda adopted in 2015 "attends to the 'unfinished business' of the EFA agenda and the education-related MDGs, and addresses global and national education challenges" (UNESCO 2015c: §5). However, if past progress rates continue into the future, in low-income countries universal primary education will be achieved only by 2088 (UNESCO 2016). The present crisis of educational systems should encourage the development of innovative solutions able to deal with growing complexity by developing new responses and approaches to public policy. As the world makes an effort to achieve the goals envisaged by the Education 2030 agenda, a "fundamental change of mindsets [is] needed to trigger action for sustainable

---

[1] *Ed tech could increase inequality, experts warn*: https://www.devex.com/news/ed-tech-could-increase-inequality-experts-warn-94563.

8 Conclusion 173

development" (UNESCO 2015a: 11). The Incheon Declaration also calls for "bold and innovative actions, to reach [such an] ambitious goal by 2030" (UNESCO 2015c: 20).

This renewed global commitment may represent an opportunity for bringing about a comprehensive discussion to rethink educational governance substantially in order to address the challenges coming from the new global education scenario and to implement more effective and ethical international education policies. The challenges facing education systems worldwide may be seized as an opportunity to rethink the ways in which public institutions are organized, and for what purposes. As argued in Hursh (2016), there is a need for "(re)build[ing] those social institutions and processes that help solve our collective problems" (p. 113).

It is against this backdrop that the theoretical discussion of this work is conducted. The analysis and the re-contextualization of principles of governance appear essential in order to fully understand the policy implications resulting from the adoption of different frameworks and to identify potential strategies for innovative reforms. As illustrated in this book, the choice between an approach to education considered as a public good, or as private and marketable good, is far from irrelevant and it often brings about contrasting imaginaries and priorities with implications for public policy that vary considerably. Given the "peculiar nature" of education (Levin 2000), serving both public and private interests and purposes, public institutions are asked to find the balance between these two apparently contrasting approaches so as not to undermine the fundamental principles of equity, social justice and equality of opportunity. This choice should be made by governments and cannot be left in the hands of individuals or households who also have to deal with private needs and aspirations.

In a context of greater privatization and marketization of education, the revisited concept of education as a public good calls for the development of democratic institutions able to deal with confrontation and to favour participation in order to promote a comprehensive discussion on the foundational elements of educational policy and practice. While reaffirming the importance of the role of the State in the provision and funding of education opportunities, the greater participation of non-state actors requires that the State strengthens, above all, its regulatory function in order to preserve the public sphere. Indeed, the public sphere is certainly "under attack" as neo-liberal claims and managerial approaches have decreased this "space of criticism" especially with regard to democratic deliberation processes and principles (Apple 2006).

Despite the fact that neo-liberalism has been one of the determinant forces which has contributed to the significant economic growth in many countries, the model of development based on liberalization and on the predominance of market mechanisms has been deemed as the cause for the return of inequality to the levels existing one century ago (Mason 2015). Indeed, significant inequalities persist throughout countries worldwide. According to studies conducted by Oxfam, economic inequality is rising, with the "85 richest individuals in the world hav[ing] as much wealth as the poorest half of the global population" (Oxfam 2014: 6). More recent data also show that "the super-rich and corporations are paying lower rates of tax than they have in decades" (Oxfam 2019: 2). In addition to greater economic inequalities, unsustainable patterns of consumption and production are causing ecological stress and degradation, with negative consequences for livelihood and stability in many countries (UNESCO 2015b). For these reasons, the neo-liberal model appears to have failed in providing sustainable solutions for social and human well-being (Mason 2015). By undermining equality and social justice, marketization puts the functioning of healthy democratic systems itself at risk.

Restructuring the *public* depends on a strong political will which aims at revisiting those rules that have favoured the expansion of market ideologies at the expense of equality and democracy. Since market alone cannot exist without an explicit state intervention, it is important to understand which rules are being implemented and which norms, values and systems of power, these rules reflect. As argued by many scholars, the challenge is not merely about the choice between the State and the market but an essential issue of democracy which concerns both the quality of the State and of the market (Reich 2015; Apple 2006; Hursh 2016).

With regard to education, the way the public sphere should be reconstituted requires a radical change in the approach to education policy and practices. A simple defence of the public sector is not useful to counterbalance the distortive effects of privatization in the field of education (Ball 2007; Burch 2009). Indeed, the effects of economic market-driven approaches have had a significant impact on education, "since the point was reached when money, having become all-powerful, changed cultural and moral attitudes" (UNESCO 1993: 1).[2] The response to privatization "cannot be based on the simple assertion that everything we now have has to be defended" (Apple 2006: 119). To address the long-standing crisis in education systems, it has been argued that there is need for a shift in culture, a transformative change in order to significantly revisit and reshape the way of functioning of public institutions themselves (UNESCO 2016; Hursh 2016; Tedesco 1995).

For this change to be possible and practicable, minimum and enabling conditions are necessary. First and foremost, there should be democratically established public institutions and a political environment which favours both participation and accountability. This not only depends largely on agreement and a strong political will but, in order to introduce new approaches and perspectives able to deal with change and complexity, also on the need to have "accurate diagnoses concerning the current situation, a considerable amount of information concerning global trends and mechanisms for evaluating the actions undertaken" (Tedesco 1995: 110).

The contribution of all actors is increasingly indispensable in order to promote the development of democratic institutions able to innovate and identify more structured responses to the crisis of educational systems. Indeed, it has been shown that the adoption of market mechanisms and the provision of standardized solutions to the problems facing education worldwide may lead to forms of exclusion and discrimination.

8.1 The Arguments Discussed in This Book

It has been illustrated that building constructive and sustainable alternatives requires education to be considered not only as a public good but also as a common good. Indeed, the concept of common goods may help to develop new approaches that are able to integrate the notion of education as a public good with the fundamental social and cultural components of education in order to enhance a transformative and alternative system

---

[2] For more details regarding UNESCO's humanism, see: Elfert (2015).

of governance that promotes education not only as an economic tool for individual progress but above all as a collective endeavour for the fulfilment of human beings and of their communities. It is suggested that a change is needed in the way in which public and governmental power is used for the promotion of a greater complementation of both top-down and bottom-up approaches.

As illustrated throughout this book, building on alternative practices which oppose the processes of privatization and marketization, the notion of common goods promotes the development of instruments of participatory democracy and puts greater emphasis on the networks of solidarity among citizens and groups. It is about suggesting a transformation of public institutions through greater participation of citizens in the introduction of viable policies and practices in order to overcome more utilitarian and individualistic approaches and build more democratic schooling systems. As argued by Hursh (2016).

> we need to develop democratic processes that place educators, parents, and students in the center of decision making. Such changes will require more than protesting the neoliberal agenda; it will also necessitate developing new social structures. (p. 107)

Having said this, it has also been suggested that the principle of education as a common good does not propose easy solutions since it depends on a strong political commitment, willing to call into question current cultural models and institutions in order to promote innovation and social change based on the values of human dignity and freedom. More structured and innovative responses to the challenges facing educational systems need to be carefully designed and require trust in the democratic functioning of institutions. Indeed, unlike corporate reforms which tend to reduce the spaces of participation, new responses which build on the concept of education as a common good, and which can see people taking more responsibility, need to be based both on trust and community, and this can be more easily achieved in those contexts where the principles of equality and equity are safeguarded (Hursh 2016).

The role of civil society is crucial in the development of alternatives that take into consideration the diversity of contexts. The contribution of civil society organizations at all levels of the education endeavour may help in the analysis of current realties and in the monitoring of education policies. Their role is essential in enabling the voices of all citizens to be heard and in influencing the functioning of public institutions. Strengthening partnerships with civil society organizations would mean that governments would have the possibility of developing public education systems that take into consideration both innovation and inclusion. Indeed, it is widely acknowledged that when the public sector accepts and integrates different contributions in order to innovate and invest in the quality of education, it is generally preferred over the private sector.

It has also been argued that the concept of education as a common good should favour a humanistic vision of education and the enhancement of the cultural and social dimensions of each educational process while promoting innovative pedagogies. With regard to the private sector, this feature requires that corporate actors replace mere for-profit market logics with social objectives (Bruni 2012). Private actors should be called on to manage educational services in both an ethical and a sustainable manner without profit representing the only motivation. It requires the establishment of forms of cooperation that replace the logics of economic competition. This does not mean prohibiting all kinds of profit to private actors, but it means creating a system of accountability and control whereby profit is made in the full respect of social and environmental sustainability. It is about rediscovering the ethical underpinnings of economic theory itself, grounded in social relationships more than in economic transactions and profit-making purposes (Becchetti et al. 2019; Bruni 2012).

A shift in the relationships of current arrangements of power between the private corporate sector and public institutions is therefore required in order to develop forms of cooperation based on partnerships that favour the many, not the few (Reich 2015). Indeed, when "genuinely based on exchange and mutual benefit", partnerships may contribute to the development of a new form of cooperation (Delors et al. 1996: 183).

The private sector may have an important role in society as long as it is able to work with citizens and public institutions in the development of new ways to achieve shared societal goals. This is based on the acknowledgment that viable solutions are those which are culturally and socially

178   R. Locatelli

fair. The closure of the for-profit chain of low-fee private schools in Uganda and Kenya which happened over the last few years is a clear sign that when education solutions are designed and developed without the direct involvement of citizens, teachers, parents and students, the final result is far from sustainable and acceptable both in economic and socio-cultural terms. The recently adopted Abidjan Principles[3] identify and examine the existing obligations of States under international human rights law to provide quality public education and to regulate private involvement in education. In the same spirit, a resolution recently adopted by the European Parliament also considers that it is a requirement under human rights law and a necessity for the achievement of the Sustainable Development Goals that the European Union refrains from funding commercial private schools.[4]

It is necessary to acknowledge the positive contributions that private actors may provide, while also paying increasing attention to the limitations and challenges of private involvement in the education sector. As stated by Minow (2003), "the preconditions for a constitutional democracy are also its stated values; a population with the freedom and equality to pursue self-governance is both the end and the means of democratic political systems. [The involvement of non-state actors] could either undermine this alignment of ends and means or strengthen it and the values of pluralism and freedom it pursues" (p. 1270).

8.2   The Role of International Cooperation in Education

For structured and viable alternatives to be sustainable, it is necessary that both the national and global levels are aligned to a vision of education seen as a public and common good. Indeed, it is widely acknowledged

---

[3] The *Abidjan Principles on the human rights obligations of States to provide public education and to regulate private involvement in education* are available at the following link: https://www.abidjan-principles.org/.

[4] European Parliament resolution of 13 November 2018 on EU development assistance in the field of education http://www.europarl.europa.eu/sides/getDoc.do?pubRef=-//EP//TEXT+TA+P8-TA-2018-0441+0+DOC+XML+V0//EN.

that there is a progressive shift in the locus of decision-making from the State to the global level with the constitution of complex global governance arrangements. This study suggests that the concept of education as a global common good may call for the adoption of a cultural shift also regarding international cooperation in the field of education.

At this particular historical moment, organizations such as UNESCO can play a leading role as public international institutions, representing most of the States of the world in fostering the establishment of mechanisms that can monitor and facilitate the implementation of policies that favour a humanistic approach and the democratic governance of education. Leading the global agenda for education, UNESCO is in a privileged position to facilitate international cooperation in education based on a vision of education seen as a common good. Indeed, "the common good is a typical UNESCO concept as it has a long tradition in all cultures".[5]

Democratic governance at the global level can be strengthened by the participation of governments and other global actors able to identify, protect and enhance different visions of development. Indeed, international civil society organizations, as well as popular movements, are playing an increasingly influential role in global arenas. These actors may be able to seize the voice of the most vulnerable and marginalized people, boosting the values of social justice, equity and solidarity among human beings. Moreover, cooperation among universities and research centres worldwide could help identify new structures and arrangements necessary for the realization of these alternative visions in different contexts "to furthering the cause of the knowledge democracy" (Biesta 2007: 469).

All these factors are necessary to define a societal project open to the contributions of all cultures, knowing that common development is the result of the cooperation among diverse worldviews, systems of knowledge and experiences. Education as a global common good implies an effective and substantial democratic governance at the global level, based on the adoption of a different cultural perspective on issues that affect us all.

---

[5] Maren Elfert. *Rethinking Education: Towards a Global Common Good? UNESCO's New Humanistic Manifesto?* 23 December 2015. NORRAG Blog. Available at this link: https://www.norrag.org/rethinking-education-towards-a-global-common-good-unescos-new-humanistic-manifesto/.

8.3 Addressing Inequality

Given the complexity of the subject in question, this work has strived to provide more clarity with regard to the use and significance of important concepts that drive the formulation of educational policies. As discussed in the introduction, theoretical critical analysis contributes to a better understanding of the issues that are behind the adoption of specific concepts. This study can be included in the type of "research *of* policy" (Desjardins and Rubenson 2009), which does not directly aim at offering concrete solutions for the formulation of policies but at least clarifies the meanings and implications that may arise from the adoption of different policy frameworks.

It has been argued that there is an unprecedented need to strengthen the role of the State at this time of increasing involvement of non-state actors at all levels of the education endeavour. The analysis of the concept of education as a public good has tried to provide greater clarity on the roles and functions of public institutions, in not only the provision and funding of education opportunities but also with regard to the regulatory and monitoring roles which are becoming even more essential for the democratic governance of education systems. The State is determinant for the elaboration of alternative frameworks that encourage cooperation among state and non-state actors, indicating a particular vision of education that is also a political project for a democratic society, in contrast to a vision of education serving individual economic interests.

This analysis has also tried to expand theory and thinking by identifying new frameworks that may inspire the adoption of innovative visions more relevant to the diversity of contexts and needs of societies worldwide. Indeed, besides revisiting and reaffirming education as a public good, it is also argued that the concept of common goods may contribute to the advancement and rethinking of democratic public institutions. The effects of neo-liberal policies driven merely by market approaches to education have to be dealt with and complemented by more structured responses that build on the forces of society and empower them to become actively involved in the process of education policy formulation and implementation. This is necessary in order to build systems that are sustainable and therefore inclusive and equitable.

In his book *The Great Leveler* (2017), the historian Walter Scheidel demonstrates that, throughout world history, only violence and catastrophes have consistently reduced inequality. According to Scheidel, mass-mobilization warfare, transformative revolutions, state collapse and catastrophic plagues represent the main factors of levelling which have repeatedly destroyed the fortunes of the rich and contributed to the reduction of wealth inequalities in societies. In this rapidly changing world, where the pace of technological innovation is evolving at an unprecedented rate and economic inequalities are rising, it is increasingly important to address educational and cultural inequalities (Calenda 2018). Indeed, economic equality cannot be achieved if there is no cultural and educational equality. Education and the whole stock of cultural and humanistic knowledge represent the necessary tools for ensuring the democratic functioning of welfare systems. However, just as liberal democracy has aimed at protecting the freedom of individuals from the tyranny of the majority, a new progressive democracy is now needed, one which not only aims at protecting freedom but also re-builds an innovative sense of community, based on the idea that the harmonious development of society is of benefit for all.

In a context of growing privatization and marketization both *of* and *in* education (Ball and Youdell 2008), there is a need to reframe education not only as a public but also as a common good. It has been argued that greater public intervention and regulation is required in the field of education, since this is the prerequisite for any action taken in view of ensuring more inclusive and democratic governance. At the same time, it has also been argued that, in order to address the influence of the market in both private and public domains, it is necessary to significantly revisit and reshape the way public institutions themselves function. The concept of education as a common good may contribute to the identification of innovative and democratic solutions based on a vision of education seen not merely as an economic tool but mainly as the process through which human beings and communities fully develop. Education can contribute either to the worsening of inequalities—when considered as a means of indoctrination or mass control—or to their reduction, by promoting greater awareness, participation and freedom. Governments and communities have the capacity to reshape and innovate current social structures so that education may represent a "positive leveller" to ensure that a sustainable future is available for all people worldwide.

References

Apple, M. W. (2006). *Educating the "Right" Way: Markets, Standards, God and Inequality* (2nd ed.). New York: Routledge.

Ball, S. J. (2007). *Education PLC*. London: Routledge.

Ball, S. J., & Youdell, D. (2008). *Hidden Privatisation in Public Education*. Brussels: Education International.

Becchetti, L., Bruni, L., & Zamagni, S. (2019). *Economia civile e sviluppo sostenibile: Progettare e misurare un nuovo modello di benessere*. Roma: Ecra Edizioni.

Biesta, G. (2007). Towards the Knowledge Democracy? Knowledge Production and the Civic Role of the University. *Studies in Philosophy and Education, 26*(5), 467–479.

Bruni, L. (2012). *Le nuove virtù del mercato nell'era dei beni comuni*. Roma: Città Nuova.

Burch, P. (2009). *Hidden Markets. The New Education Privatization*. London: Routledge.

Calenda, C. (2018). *Orizzonti Selvaggi: Capire la paura e ritrovare il coraggio*. Milano: Feltrinelli Editore.

Delors, J., et al. (1996). *Learning: The Treasure Within*. Report to UNESCO of the International Commission on Education for the Twenty-First Century. Paris: UNESCO.

Desjardins, R., & Rubenson, K. (2009). *Research of vs Research for Education Policy—In an Era of Transnational Policy-Making*. Saarbrücken: VDM Verlag Dr. Müller.

Elfert, M. (2015, December 23). *Rethinking Education: Towards a Global Common Good? UNESCO's New Humanistic Manifesto?* NORRAG NEWSBite. Retrieved from https://norrag.wordpress.com/2015/12/23/rethinking-education-towards-a-global-common-good-unescos-new-humanistic-manifesto.

Hursh, D. W. (2016). *The End of Public Schools. The Corporate Reform Agenda to Privatize Education*. New York: Routledge.

Levin, H. M. (2000). *The Public-Private Nexus in Education: Occasional Paper No. 1*. New York: National Center for the Study of Privatization in Education.

Mason, P. (2015). *Postcapitalism: A Guide to Our Future*. London: Penguin Books.

Minow, M. (2003). Public and Private Partnerships: Accounting for the New Religion. *Harvard Law Review, 116*(5), 1229–1270.

Oxfam. (2014). *Working for the Many: Public Services Fight Inequality*. Oxfam Briefing Paper, 182(3).

Oxfam. (2019, January). *Public Good or Private Wealth?* Oxfam Briefing Paper.

Reich, R. (2015). *Saving Capitalism: For the Many, Not the Few*. New York: Alferd Knopf.

Scheidel, W. (2017). *The Great Leveler: Violence and the History of Inequality from the Stone Age to the Twenty-First Century*. Princeton, NJ: Princeton University Press.

Tedesco, J. C. (1995). *The New Educational Pact: Education, Competitiveness and Citizenship in Modern Society*. Geneva: IBE-UNESCO.

UNESCO. (1993, March 2–4). *EDC/2. International Commission on Education for the 21st Century*. First Session. UNESCO Headquarters, Paris. EDC.93/CONF.001/I.7 REV. Paris: UNESCO Archives.

UNESCO. (2015a). *World Education Forum 2015—Final Report*. Paris: UNESCO.

UNESCO. (2015b). *Rethinking Education: Towards a Global Common Good?* Paris: UNESCO.

UNESCO. (2015c). *Education 2030 Incheon Declaration and Framework for Action*. Paris: UNESCO.

UNESCO. (2016). *Education for People and Planet: Creating Sustainable Futures for All*. Global Education Monitoring Report 2016. Paris: UNESCO.

UNESCO. (2018). *Migration, Displacement and Education: Building Bridges, Not Walls*. Global Education Monitoring Report 2019. Paris: UNES.

Index[1]

A

Abidjan Principles, 23
Access plus learning, 71
Accountability, 53, 76, 132
Accountability mechanisms, 138
Active citizenship, 139
Aid to education, 152
Approach, 141
Arab States, 65
Arendt, Hannah, 137
Average duration of schooling, 69
Awareness, 139, 182

B

Basic learning levels, 72
Benefits, 130
Blurring of boundaries, 3

Bottom-up approaches, 133, 176
Bridge International Academies, 80
Business, 46, 74

C

Calculus of care, 73
Capability approach, 140
Caribbean, 65
Charter schools, 54
Citizens, 12
Civil society, 130
Civil society organizations, 46
Classification of public goods, 36
Collective endeavour, 112, 139
Collective shared endeavour, 143
Commercialisation, 24

---

[1] Note: Page numbers followed by 'n' refer to notes.

© The Author(s) 2019
R. Locatelli, *Reframing Education as a Public and Common Good,*
https://doi.org/10.1007/978-3-030-24801-7

186   Index

Committee on the Rights of the Child, 17
Commodification, 28
Commodity, 21, 24, 73
Common good, 11, 118, 119
Common property resources, 119
Common-pool resources, 119
Common societal endeavour, 129
Commons, 118, 122
Community, 139
Community engagement, 11
Community organizations, 131
Community participation, 131
Community partnerships, 133
Competition, 74, 134
Competitiveness, 21
Compulsory, 8
Compulsory education, 2, 44
Conceptions of development, 167
Constitutional democracy, 178
Consumable good, 3
Consumer choice, 21
Consumers, 73, 130
Convergent goods, 124
Cooperation, 122
Co-participation, 130
Co-production, 130
Corporate or individual interests, 81
Corporations, 174
Corruption, 72
Criteria of publicness, 11, 91
Critical citizenship, 81
Critical thinking, 109
Cultural traditions, 167
Culture of democracy, 141
Curriculum, 107
Curriculum development, 62
Curriculum standards, 101

D

Decision-making process, 53, 106
Decomposable, 124
Definition of public and private, 61
Degradation, 174
Degree of regulation, 58
Deliberate cooperation, 166
Delors, Jacques, 17
Delors Commission, 26
Delors Report, 17
Democracy, 5, 105
Democratic educational governance, 15
Democratic governance, 83
Democratic participation, 11, 42
Democratic policy-making, 10
Democratic system, 111
Demographic changes, 64, 69
De-professionalization of teachers, 81
Deregulation, 53, 93
Development discourse, 15
Dignity, 129
Discrimination, 134
Distribution of teachers, 71
Diversification of sources of financing, 46, 59
Diversified demand for education, 68
Diversity, 129
Dominant development discourse, 12, 150

E

Ecological stress, 174
Economic approach, 29
Economic challenge, 38
Economic crisis, 70

Index 187

Economic discourse, 21
Economic events, 37
Economic growth, 174
Economic inequality, 174
Economic theory, 33
Economic theory of public goods, 27
Edu-businesses, 76
Educational and cultural inequalities, 181
Educational governance, 3
Education as a common good, 11, 12, 127, 149
Education as a human right, 80, 153
Education as a public good, 11, 157
The Education Commission, 98
Education for All, 4, 6, 9
Education for All—Fast Track Initiative, 24
Education International, 23
Education multilateralism, 155
Education policy, 29
Education policy discourse, 8
Education privatization, 10
Education technologies, 172
Education 2030 agenda, 1
Educators, 130
Eecke, Wilfried Ver, 37
Efficiency, 74
Empowerment, 139, 144
Endogenous, 53
Equality, 2, 22
Equitable access, 132
Equity, 2, 10, 22
European Parliament, 178
European Union, 178
Examinations, 62
Excess demand, 68
Excludable and rivalrous good, 39

Exclusion, 134
Exogenous, 53
Expansion of access to education, 69
Expansion of education, 52
Expansion of the public domain, 46, 156

F

Failure of governments, 4, 52
Failure of public education systems, 26
Families, 130
Financial crisis, 129
Flexibility, 132
Formal, 140
Formal democracy, 136
Formal education constitutes a public good, 144
Formal factors, 105
For-profit education, 2, 3, 45
Fragile countries, 171
Framework for Action, 1, 18
Free, 6
Freedom, 110, 128
Free market, 35
Free-rider problem, 35
Functional conditions, 107–109
Funding, 45, 66, 99

G

General Agreement on Trade in Services, 79
General interest, 129
Global Campaign for Education, 24
Global common goods, 12
Global education agenda, 166

188 Index

Global Education Industry, 6, 79
Global governance, 149
Global governance arrangements, 179
Global governance of education, 12, 155
Global Initiative for Economic, Social and Cultural Rights, 23
Globalization, 3, 73, 154
Global Multistakeholder Partnerships in Education, 163–164
Global Partnership for Education, 9, 16, 24
Global public goods, 149
Global South, 6
Global trade, 79
Global understanding, 159
Governance, 4, 10, 51
Governing the commons, 121
Government failure, 70
Growing demands for education, 64

H

Hardin, Garrett, 119
Higher education, 9
Higher education as a public good, 20
Homo economicus, 129
Horizontal, 136
Households, 46
Human capital, 3, 21
Human capital theory, 74
Human dignity, 128
Humanistic and integrated vision of education, 26
Humanistic approach, 6, 11, 144

Humanistic economy, 134
Humanistic vision, 11
Human rights, 1
Human Rights Council, 17
Human rights treaty bodies, 9
Human togetherness, 110

I

Illiterate adults, 172
Immaterial resources, 118
Impure public goods, 35
Incheon Declaration on Education 2030, 18
Inclusion, 2
Incomplete schooling, 70
Indigenous communities, 171
Indirect costs, 46
Individual benefits, 25
Individual private and consumable good, 75
Informal education, 140
Innovation, 74
Innovative pedagogies, 177
Inspection, 62
Instrumental role, 27
Instrumental vision, 12
Integrated approach, 11, 140, 144
Integration, 130
Internally displaced people, 171
International Commission on Financing Global Education Opportunity, 151
International cooperation in education, 155
International Covenant on Economic, Social and Cultural Rights, 44

Index   **189**

International Monetary Fund (IMF), 78
International public institutions, 164
International trade in education services, 21
Investment, 3
Isomorphism, 154

J

Jomtien World Conference, 133

K

Knowledge democracy, 179
Knowledge systems, 129, 140

L

Lack of accountability, 72
Latin America, 65
Learning crisis, 71
Levels of interpretation, 15
Liberal economic approach, 74
Liberalization, 3, 54
Lifelong learning, 139
Literacy, 71
Literacy rate, 151, 172
Logics of property, 125
Low-fee private schools, 6, 80

M

Marginalized, 179
Marginalized children, 70
Marketable, 3
Market control, 75
Market economics, 51

Market failures, 35
Market mechanisms, 3, 9
Marketization, 29, 74
Material resources, 118
Mathematics, 172
Mercantalization of education, 21
Merit good, 39
Migrants, 171
Millennium Development Goals, 4, 9
Minorities, 171
Mismanagement, 72
Monitoring functions, 100
Multifaceted phenomenon of privatization, 8
Multilateral organizations, 152
Multiplication of public and private actors, 59
Multi-stakeholder, 141
Musgrave, Richard, 2, 34
Mutual accountability, 134

N

Narrowing the curriculum, 108
National Education Accounts (NEA) methodology, 66
Nation-state, 15
Nature of education, 4, 11
NEA analysis, 67
Neoclassical economic theory, 28
Neo-liberal, 6, 11
Neo-liberal ideology, 51, 52, 73
Neo-liberalism, 73
Network State, 152
New Public Management, 76
NGOs, 9
Non-discrimination, 22

190 Index

Non-excludability, 34
Non-formal, 140
Non-rivalry, 34
Non-state actors, 2
Normative principle, 28
Numeracy skills, 71

O
Organisation for Economic
Co-operation and
Development (OECD), 9, 25
Ostrom, Elinor, 121
Out-of-school children, 150
Outsourcing of services, 46, 53
Ownership, 45

P
Paradigm change, 134
Parents, 131
Participation, 6, 107
Participatory accountability, 138
Participatory democracy, 11, 122, 136
Participatory process, 129
Pedagogy, 107
Peers, 131
Performance, 132
Philanthropic organizations, 51–52
Pluralism, 178
Policy focus, 9, 27
Policy framework, 180
Political activity, 110
Political commitment, 128
Political economy, 40–41
Polycentric governance, 158
Poor quality education, 70
Popular movements, 179
Popular sovereignty, 141

Post-2015 education agenda, 18
Power, 137
Principles of governance, 9, 27, 173
Private, 2, 3
Private engagement, 6
Private institution, 60
Private involvement, 15
Private markets, 26
Private profit, 24
Private providers, 53
Private schooling, 53
Private sector, 3, 130
Private-good aspects, 94
Privatization, 2, 122
Privatization in public education,
53
Privatization of public education,
53
Process of privatization, 53
Progressive democracy, 181
Provision, 45, 99
Public, 3
Public accountability, 111, 163
Public and private sphere, 4
Public education, 22, 42
Public financing, 2
Public funds, 25
Public good, 1
Public-good aspects, 26, 95
Public institution, 60
Public interest, 2, 5, 19
Public international institutions,
179
Publicness, 111, 156
Public–private partnerships (PPPs),
6, 54, 162
Public responsibility, 19
Public schooling system, 42
Public service, 21

Index **191**

Public sphere, 11, 46
Pure public goods, 35
Purposes of education, 4, 51

Q

Qualification function, 108
Quality, 6, 132
Quality assurance mechanisms,
101
Quasi-market, 76

R

Rates of return, 3
Rationales, 10
Reading, 172
Refugees, 171
Regulation, 45, 53, 58
Regulatory framework, 21
Regulatory function, 100
Relational approach, 143
Relational conception of human
rights, 125
Relational goods, 125
Relational process, 41
Relationships, 129
Res communes, 119
Research centres, 179
Researchers, 130
Research for policy, 8
Research of policy, 8
Responsibility, 139
Rethinking Education: Towards a
global common good,
27–28
Right to education, 2, 43
Right to Education Initiative, 23
Right to lifelong learning, 139

Right to quality education, 18
Risks, 130
Role of the state, 2, 4, 6, 33

S

Samuelson, Paul, 2, 34
School choice, 82
Schooling, 9, 21
SDG-Education 2030 Steering
Committee, 19
Shared action, 124
Shared governance, 130
Shared responsibility, 134, 158
Shift in culture, 112, 142
Significance of education, 111
Singh, Kishore, 21
Social cohesion, 42
Social commitment, 132
Social connection model, 139
Social construct, 36
Social changes, 64
Social development, 27
Socialization, 109
Social justice, 10, 164
Social relations, 129
Social structures, 176
Societal/collective purposes of
education, 10
Societal good, 47
Solidarity, 129, 179
South Asia, 64
Special Rapporteurs on the Right to
Education, 16
State, 46
State intervention, 40
Steering Committee, 164, 166
Structural Adjustment Programs
(SAPs), 78

192   Index

Students, 130
Subjectification functions, 109
Sub-Saharan Africa, 65
Subsidiarity, 136
Sustainability, 161
Sustainable Development Goal 4, 2

T

Tax avoidance, 72
Teacher absenteeism, 132
Teacher accountability, 73
Teachers, 130
Teachers' unions, 23
Teacher training, 132
Teaching to the test, 108
Technological innovation, 181
Think tanks, 153
Tomaševski, Katarina, 20
Tooley, James, 79
Top-down, 176
The Tragedy of the Commons, 119
Transnational corporations, 153
Transparent communication, 107
Trends of education privatization, 29

U

UN Committee on Economic, Social
    and Cultural Rights, 17
UN Interagency Task Force on
    Financing for Development
    affirms, 151
UN Special Rapporteur, 21
UNESCO, 9
UNESCO Global Education
    Monitoring Report, 138
UNESCO International Institute for
    Educational Planning, 60

UNESCO Institute for Statistics, 61
Unfinished business, 172
UNICEF, 9
United Nations, 16
United Nations Development
    Programme (UNDP), 156
Universal Declaration of Human
    Rights, 22
Universal primary education, 63,
    171
Universal Responsibility, 159n7
Universities, 179
Users, 130
Utilitarian approaches, 17, 29

V

Vertical, 136
Vision of education, 9
Vouchers, 53
Voucher scheme, 54, 75
Vulnerable, 179

W

Washington Consensus, 78
Welfare state, 52
Welfare system, 128, 131
West Asia, 64
Wheel of welfare, 56
World Bank, 9, 25
World Conference on EFA, 17
World Conference on Higher
    Education, 20
World culture values, 167
World Education Forum, 23
World Trade Organization's (WTO),
    79
Worldviews, 129